AN ANGLICAN VIEW
OF
THE VATICAN COUNCIL

An Anglican View
of the
Vatican Council

By the Reverend
BERNARD C. PAWLEY
Canon of Ely

MOREHOUSE-BARLOW CO.
NEW YORK

First American Edition, 1962

PRINTED AND BOUND IN THE UNITED STATES OF AMERICA

PREFACE

A GREAT deal has been said by Roman Catholics about their forthcoming Vatican Council; the Lutherans also have made some appraisals, and there have been a few symposia. When the author of this present contribution suggested that someone should survey the situation from the Anglican point of view, he did not expect that his idea would be bounced back to himself, but that is what happened. There was a time when to "stick one's neck out" in the field of Christian unity could be a risky, if not painful, experience. Now, with thanks to the Holy Spirit, anyone can be confident that when a belief is held in good faith it can be declared and received with forbearance and courtesy.

The author owes thanks to the Bishop of Ely and to his colleagues the Dean and Chapter of Ely for leaves of absence in Rome; to the Rev. G. W. H. Lampe, the Rev. E. L. Mascall, and Sir Will Spens for advice and encouragement (though they have no responsibility for opinions expressed); to the Rector (the Rev. Wilbur C. Woodhams) and Vestry of St. Paul's (American) Parish, Rome, for hospitality and much kindness; to the Rev. D. J. N. Wanstall and the congregation of All Saints', Rome, for encouragement; and to his wife for help in typing the manuscript. He also salutes the large number of people who, from inside the Roman Catholic Church, are working for new relations, in particular His Eminence Cardinal Béa and the staff of the Secretariat for Promoting Christian Union and, in England, Msgr. J. C. Heenan, the Roman Catholic Archbishop of Liverpool; and there is no one whose writings show more evidence of a real effort to understand the problems than the Rev. Bernard Leeming, S.J., of Heythrop.

Except insofar as others are quoted and acknowledged, this book expresses only the opinions of its author; it is in no sense an official document of the Church of England, still less of the Anglican Communion.

BERNARD C. PAWLEY

Ely, 1962

CONTENTS

AN ANGLICAN VIEW
OF
THE VATICAN COUNCIL

1

CHURCH UNITY

THIS book is written not for specialists, but for ordinary well-intentioned churchmen, who have begun to respond to God's promptings that Christians of this generation should seek again the unity in Christ which, down through the centuries, has been lost. Enthusiasm can often be fired by information, and information in this case concerns the Second Vatican Council of the Roman Catholic Church, 1962, the motives which have prompted it, the questions it hopes to solve, and the possible effects it may have on Christian churches in general and upon the world at large. To do that adequately, the reader must have, in brief form, some facts about present-day relations between the Roman Catholic Church and other Christian bodies, and an even shorter, and perhaps less adequate account of the origins of those broken relations; he must also see the Council in the light of other Christian gatherings and plannings for the unity of Christian churches throughout the world.

The effort of Christians to seek unity is now so widespread and familiar as to be in danger of becoming commonplace—widespread, that is, among both the clergy and the laity; it is not, however, something which can be said to have gripped the imagination of the majority of Christians. That is perhaps largely because the average Christian, while giving assent to the principle that all Christians should be one, is not yet convinced that ecclesiastical superiors really believe the ideal possible of realization.

Laymen are more perceptive than the clergy usually give them credit: they agree that disunity is scandalous, they hear

1

exhortations to seek unity, they observe spasmodic efforts which are promoted to that end—exchange of pulpits, meetings of local councils of churches, occasional news of a merger—but they perceive, in a healthy non-professional way, that there is not sufficient willingness to change old habits, to try new ways of worship, or to adopt old ones; and that for real unity to be established, century-old divisions and prejudices must be worn down.

Gradually undeniable facts of progress and achievement have been changing the situation. Schemes for union have been proposed, argued about, and actually carried through— some at a safe distance, but gradually they occur nearer at home.

The World Council of Churches, whose meetings now receive wide publicity, is evidence that at least some Christians mean business. Until 1959 there was a serious hindrance to the development of Christian thinking and activity in matters pertaining to Christian unity which was by no means so evident to the specialists as it was to those who relied on the principle of common sense: for until that time there were many who were zealous for the unity of Christendom but who left the Roman Catholic Church completely out of the picture.

It will of course be claimed that this was never so and that all proponents of Christian unity desired nothing better than that the Roman Catholic Church should join the move towards unity and should in fact become a member of the World Council of Churches; but for many it was not even considered remotely possible, and for many more it was not even thought desirable. The Christian world was therefore confronted with an extraordinary spectacle of people desiring and working for Christian unity, as they conceived it, who nevertheless failed to consider more than half of Christendom in their schemes. The insufficiency and inconsist-

ency of the omission was evident to more people than was
at the time suspected, and was undoubtedly one of the
causes why laymen did not respond with enthusiasm to the
various proposals.

To that era of limited vision and work for Christian unity
the events of 1959 and 1960 put a deliberate end, for it was
in 1959 that Pope John XXIII announced the Second Vatican Council, which would be held with "the promoting of
union among all Christian peoples" in mind, and in 1960 the
Archbishop of Canterbury, then Geoffrey Fisher, paid his
well-known visit to the Pope. Though neither of the two
events by themselves could be said to have accomplished
much in a practical way to further the unity of Christians,
yet psychologically and spiritually their importance cannot
be overestimated, for, despite any official disclaimers, they
gave the lie to any conception of ultimate unity in which the
Roman Catholic portion of Christendom was not entirely
involved.

Now that the view has been so greatly enlarged, we may
consider the matter decisively: local and limited search for
Christian unity is not enough, and, further, union is an absolute, and not a relative, term. To be working, say, for the
amalgamation of the Church of England with the other
churches in England while retaining centuries-old prejudices and ignorance about the Roman Catholics in England
and all over the world, and retaining feelings of scepticism
about the possibility of relations with them, is not working for
unity at all. It could even be a form of self-indulgence amount-
ing to no more than seeking fellowship with those with
whom one seems to agree, and ignoring all others, and that
too is no path to unity.

For unity is that dimension of the Church's life in which
all her members seek and find their total oneness in Christ.
Even those who declare a belief in unity in its widest sense

and yet claim to be "specializing in the branch about which they know the most" need to be kept aware of those insidious dangers. Regroupings of Christian bodies by themselves are not necessarily steps toward unity.

A parallel is to be found in the present world situation: alliances of the nations of the free world have to some degree served only to deepen the isolation of the communist bloc by the building of a brick wall at the Brandenburg gate, intensifying the cold war, increasing political mistrust and economic isolation, with the ever-present possibility of war, and worse. Looking back, many doubt if the policies pursued have been as wise as they might have been. True, the banner unfurled has been the rallying one of freedom, but freedom is only one of many political "goods"; there were perhaps other groupings, other ways of living-and-let-live which might not have led to such an impasse.

The point is that those concerned with ecclesiastical oneness (and that should include every baptized Christian) should remember that ideally the Church is one and indivisible, in truth, in unity, in love. Local and confessional abstractions from that wholeness can be dangerous because of the half-truths they hold to.

Even in considering ecclesiastical organic unity we must always, in every detail, keep the ultimate end in view. Magazines and newspapers which carried the headlines "Union achieved in South India" and "Union in sight in Ceylon," and even the promoters of what is called "The Plan of Church Union in North India and Pakistan," do grievous violence to the plain meaning of words. No union has been achieved, but only a grouping of some Christian bodies, in some cases only minor and marginal ones; in every case the main body of Christians, mostly Roman Catholics were not included in the plan.

In those areas real union has not been accomplished. Work

for real union may now begin, and new groupings may perhaps (though not certainly) help; all depends on keeping right perspective in their new affiliations on how they retain or encourage the development of the main elements of catholic Christendom, and on how they regard the partial unity already achieved.

The lack of perspective and proportion in planning, the lack of vision and faith in even the possibility of real unity, the willingness to accept only portions of the whole have been characteristic of the first phase of this century's steps towards Christian unity and the chief cause of their failure. That is not to say that there has been no attempt made to include the Roman Catholic Church in the picture: in fact many pointed out the absurdity of unity without it, and in many unofficial ways and in relatively obscure places faithful members of Anglican and Roman communions have been exchanging views and visits.

Indeed, the Church of England, sensitive of its closer hold on what is known as the catholic inheritance of Christendom, has had its unofficial emissaries in many places on the continent of Europe. The great liturgical revival in the Roman Catholic Church, beginning with the inspiration at Maria Laach in Germany, has not been without Anglican sympathizers and admirers, for they have seen therein a new hope for the future—not just because of liturgical simplifications, but because of a new and deep study of biblical theology which could surely, under the hand of God, lead to better things.

While there were those who maintained contact with the Roman Catholic Church on the Continent, the situation in England was far from desirable: for in the Church of England there were two avenues of ecumenical contact, and since neither had much to do with the other, they acquired party labels. Those who were interested in and worked with the free churches were on the whole Low Church or Evangelical sympathizers, while those who maintained unofficial contacts with Roman Catholic friends on the continent of Europe were of the High Church or Catholic party. Although that division was not surprising, and in the circumstances perhaps inevitable, it was regrettable for it gave rise to hesitation, and even suspicion, on all sides; the Catholic wing was hesitant about negotiations in India, the Evangelical wing regarded suggestions of dealings with Rome as utterly impossible, the free churches got the impression that the Church of England was half-hearted, or even divided, in its dealings with them, and the Roman Catholic Church got the impression that the only hope for unity with the Church of England was to detach and absorb those who seemed able and willing to understand the concept of Catholic Christendom and forget the others. There were, of course, some who kept the whole field in view, and whose aim and purpose and sympathies were for total union.

It is against that background that we must examine Pope John XXIII's decision in 1959 to call a plenary council of the Roman Catholic Church. The Council, which will be called the Second Vatican Council, was conceived in reference to the ultimate union of all Christian peoples. It has been stated often that Christian unity is not the primary concern of the Council, and it needs repeating here to avoid misunderstanding. It is true, however, that the Council was planned to discuss, among other things, the removal, as far as possible, of barriers to unity. By itself the fact would be of no little interest, but considered with two other facts, it is a development of notable proportions.

The other facts are the setting up as part of the preparatory machinery of the Council a Secretariat for Promoting Christian Unity, in 1960, and the determination of the present Pope to show himself as a friendly and humane prelate, who is personally and keenly interested in making friends of "separated" Christians without compromising any principles of the Roman Catholic Church.

The three facts taken together form a new situation which Christians ouside the Roman Catholic Church cannot ignore. Much ink has already been put to paper in attempts to evaluate them, and, as could be expected, interpretations have been put upon them all the way from the exceedingly hopeful to the merely cynical, but it seemed to many an obvious Christian duty to accept the situation on its face value, to give thanks for it, and to respond properly.

The decision of the Archbishop of Canterbury (then Geoffrey Fisher) to pay a courtesy call on the Pope on his way back from visits to the Patriarchs of Jerusalem and Constantinople was an Anglican reaction to the new situation. The call was made on no authority of convocation nor of the Lambeth Conference, just as the Pope's decisions had been made, not as a result of long deliberation by authoritative bodies, but, as the Archbishop himself said, by inspired promptings. Archbishop Fisher's suggestion was immediately accepted by the Pope, and the history-making visit was made, not without a great amount of publicity. It is no secret that the visit caused considerable concern, and was even disapproved in some exalted Vatican circles. There is no doubt that the personality and holiness of both the Pope and the Archbishop carried the day and that the gainsayers were defeated. It was soon evident that friendliness and courtesy could take the place of coldness and indifference without compromise of principles.

From the Anglican point of view the visit was particularly felicitous because its significance was so clear. The Archbishop will long be remembered for his endeavors towards the union of Christians. His "Cambridge Sermon" at the beginning of his term of office had declared a policy which he in faith had pursued energetically and relentlessly.

In the circumstances of the time, his efforts had been necessarily directed to Christians of "free" churches, not only in England, but also in certain areas overseas, and to the World Council of Churches, in which he was always a dominating figure. There were, of course, some who feared that he might be pushing the Church of England too fast to the "left" and holding a limited conception of union. No one would have accused Archbishop Fisher of Romanophile tendencies; it was, therefore, all the more suitable and notable that it should be he who, at the end of a long episcopate (as only he then knew it to be) should make the spectacular gesture, which in the course of a few hours righted the balance of his own lifework for the union of Christians and demonstrated unmistakably that his vision for the Church was not partial but full and total and visible unity of all Christian peoples.

Officials of other churches, notably the Lutheran Bishop of Berlin, previously had paid calls on the Pope, and others have followed him, chiefly Dr. J. H. Jackson, president of the National Baptist Convention of the U.S.A., Dr. A. C. Craig, Moderator of the Church of Scotland, and the Most Rev. Arthur Lichtenberger, Presiding Bishop of the Episcopal Church in the U.S.A. Although Roman Catholic observers, even if disguised as pressmen, had been at meetings of the World Council of Churches before 1960, and were to be present openly as observers in New Delhi in 1961, it was the Archbishop's visit to Rome in November, 1960, which caught the imagination of the entire Christian world and opened up infinite, if distant, prospects of real unity. The Archbishop and Pope John XXIII will long be remembered for their historic meeting.

When Archbishop Fisher was in Rome he also visited Cardinal Béa, the German president of the new Vatican Secretariat for Unity. They agreed that before anything much could be done towards reunion of the Roman Catholic Church and Churches of the Anglican Communion, the centuries of prejudice and misunderstanding which had grown up between the two communions had to be cleared away, and it was further agreed that the start might be made in the preparations for the Second Vatican Council.

It was therefore decided to send to Rome an unofficial representative of the Archbishops of Canterbury and York whose business it should be to keep their Graces informed of the progress of the preparations for the Council, as far as they might have any bearing on the future relations between the two Churches, and to supply the Secretariat for Unity with information or answers to questions concerning the beliefs and practices of the Church of England.[1]

That representative took up his duties in 1961. He was most kindly received, was offered every facility for his work, and at the time of writing is vigorously engaged in both the above-mentioned capacities. Following the appointment it was agreed that observers shall be sent to Rome from other Churches of the Anglican Communion, as well as from the other major confessional bodies, to be present at least at some of the sessions of the Council—without, of course, the power to speak or to vote.

All these actions form a new development in inter-church relations and indicate a "thaw" in four hundred years of icy non-cooperation and even shameful hostility. The pur-

[1] In appointing a representative in the Vatican City the Archbishops of Canterbury and York did not presume to act for all Churches of the Anglican Communion, but even so they must have felt certain that their representative, however unofficial, was prepared to speak informatively of the entire communion and that the daughter Churches would watch with interest, if not approval, any developments that would ensue from his appointment and presence. Canon Pawley, the author of this book, is that representative.—ED.

pose of this book is to state briefly but clearly the main objects of the Second Vatican Council so that the new and friendly relation between the two Communions may be thoroughly understood. So important an event should certainly claim the most careful attention of Christians everywhere.

The World Council of Churches meets frequently, but the forthcoming meeting in Rome is the first full council of the Roman Catholic Church for nearly a century. The World Council is impressive for its comprehensiveness and for its ability to draw together people who hold widely different interpretations of the Christian faith. It searches for unity and encourages plans to further that end, but the Council of the Roman Catholic Church, with its representatives of every nation under the sun, can proudly declare its unity before the session opens—a most impressive exhibition of disciplined solidarity.

The Vatican Council faces other, and even more intractable, problems than that of disunity outside the Roman Catholic Church, but there is no doubt that our Roman Catholic brethren are to be admired, even envied, for having preserved so faithfully, at considerable cost, this, the first in order of the notes of Christ's Church. *Deo soli gloria;* but let those be first to give the glory who, for their own shortcomings, have lost that gift of unity, especially at a time when they are seeking to regain it.

Nevertheless it must be pointed out that if the Roman Catholic Church is satisfied with itself and if it regards the millions of Christians outside its jurisdiction as being also outside the Body of Christ, or if it plans or speaks of unity without regard to them, the unity of the Roman Catholic Church itself, which on occasion looks so impressive, is compromised and is something less than the apostolic unity for which we all long.

Those involved in the re-establishment of relations with the Roman Catholic Church, even at an unofficial level, have sensed the trust and approval which has been given to them, quietly and unobtrusively, by a majority of English churchmen; the displeased are few and have shown themselves to be isolated and extremists. English churchmen have felt instinctively that it is absurd to talk and pray about, still more to work for, union without eventually including the Roman Catholic Church. They realize that the time has come to put an end to bias and misinformation, and to face squarely, in a Christian manner, the many barriers which separate us; and, further, they wish to begin with whatever activities are common and possible without compromise of principles. Anglicans have for a long time regretted the canonical restriction which keeps Roman Catholics from praying with them in public, and now welcome with joy any change in the situation.

At the same time it is not only fair but essential to say that the present and gentler climate does not in any way mean the beginning of explorations for inter-communion, still less of negotiations to that end. Everybody feels happier when that is fully understood. The gulf which separates is too wide, misunderstandings too deep, and prejudices still too lively for this to be possible, at least on official levels, but when an opportunity such as the approaching Vatican Council presents itself, that opportunity must be fully used. Anglicans, Orthodox, Free Churchmen[2] of all nations are able to

[2] Methodists, Baptists, and the others, are called Free Church in England because they are not "established by law," as is the Church of England. In the U.S.A., Free churches are called Protestant churches. Furthermore in England, the term Protestant, as used by the Church of England, means non-papal, or non-Roman, as does the Episcopal Church in the U.S.A. when that word is used in its legal title. When the Free churches use the term, it means non-Catholic; Anglican Churches believe in a Catholic Church, not a non-Catholic church, as do the Protestants.—ED.

look towards Rome and to say "You are our brethren in
Christ. We long for unity with you in Christ, who is the
Way, the Truth, and the Life. We hear you are to hold a
Council for the renewal of your Church, for the revision of
your discipline, for the bringing up to date of doctrine and
liturgy, and to make the path of unity easier. Then let us
hear all that is in your mind. There are things which separate us, some of them grievous, but those which unite us are
greater, for do we not worship the same Lord, and share the
same baptism? In this spirit we pray that God will show us
a way out of our differences by renewing our common under-
standings of the one Faith. We ask God's blessing on your
enterprise, and pray that it may bring good to you and profit
for the whole Christian world."

This kind of dialogue, open, frank, and without illusion or
pretense, must be God's will in this matter. With the disunity of Christendom in mind, and with the forthcoming
Vatican Council as a focal point in the recovery of unity,
all Christians can honestly pray, in the words of the Gelasian
Sacramentary, as set forth in the Book of Common Prayer
and used in the days of the undivided Church:

O GRACIOUS Father, we humbly beseech thee for thy
holy Catholic Church; that thou wouldest be pleased to
fill it with all truth, in all peace. Where it is corrupt, puri-
fy it; where it is in error, direct it; where in any thing it is
amiss, reform it. Where it is right, establish it; where it
is in want, provide for it; where it is divided, reunite it;
for the sake of him who died and rose again, and ever
liveth to make intercession for us, Jesus Christ, thy Son,
our Lord. Amen.

2

PRESENT RELATIONS:
THE CHURCHES THEMSELVES

BEFORE introducing the forthcoming Vatican Council to non-Roman Catholic readers, we must consider not only what separates us from Rome, but some of the differences between the Anglican Communion and other Christian bodies. Part of the difference arises from the non-Roman Catholic side's habit of thinking of "Protestant" as a homogeneous body of people, and "Protestantism" a neat parcel of doctrine.

It cannot be denied that there is an unbelievable confusion of belief and organization among non-Roman Catholic which has been inherited from past centuries, a confusion to which, in contrast to her own international and inter-racial solidarity, the Roman Catholic Church does not hesitate to point. A further confusion arises from the various meanings of the words "catholic" and "protestant."

The Church of England, as well as other Churches of the Anglican Communion, is in a considerable difficulty here, and often seems to bestride two worlds. She is in every sense "Catholic," that is, she has received the Catholic faith and ministry in their fullness—which is why she has to speak carefully and say *Roman* Catholic to distinguish her people from those of obedience to the Church in Rome. Although she is sometimes legally described as "protestant" (non-Roman), and is proud in some respects to take her stand with non-Catholic brethren, yet to describe her as "Protestant" (non-Catholic) in the sense in which that word is understood in Europe and America is entirely misleading. Because the Reformation took an entirely different form in England than it did on the Continent our Roman Catholic brethren, to make the matter perfectly clear, are more and more making a distinction between Orthodox, Anglicans, and Protestants.

Propaganda and bias and four centuries of active conflict have wrought such havoc with Anglican-Roman Catholic relations that it is not easy even now to refer to them without danger of misunderstandings. To speak or write about them often raises the assumption that one must be "for" or "against" the Church in Rome. Today, however, the portents of the times call us clearly to discuss the relations, or the lack of them, objectively. Even well-educated members of Anglican churches are often so little acquainted with facts, that any attempt to provide information must start from elementary matters. We shall, therefore, deal only with what the two Churches say about themselves and about one another as churches, which is only part of the picture; readers from other bodies will have to make their own adjustments.

In the insular life of the Church of England (or, for that matter, the Episcopal Church in the U.S.A.) there is a tendency to think of the Roman Catholic Church as just one church, if not the oldest of all "churches," something like the "Methodist Church" or the "Presbyterian Church," but with world-wide and slightly political connotations. Visitors to an English cathedral tend to ask, "Wasn't this Roman Catholic before the Reformation?" There is no way of answering the two misconceptions except by starting at the beginning of church history with a sketch of the main events which lead up to the present situation.

The Church of the Apostles, from Pentecost onwards, was one both in spirit and in organic unity, and it was assumed that in accordance with Christ's will and explicit intention it would always remain so. Continuing in the teaching of the Apostles, Christians believed the church to be the body of Christ—a "mystery," and that belief was incorporated as an article of faith (one, holy, catholic, and apostolic church) in the creeds.

From the very beginning there have been differences and sometimes schisms. The schism of Arius, which soon followed the "liberation" of the Church, looked serious at the time but it did not endure. The creed commonly called the Nicene was the Church's answer to Arius' erratic teaching about the nature of our Lord. From the fourth century onwards, however, the Church experienced serious divisions, though none proved to be permanent until the eleventh century. The Donatist schism looked serious, but there was a reconciliation by the time of the Islamic invasions; the Monophysite movement separated most of Egypt and Syria from Constantinople; later on there was a series of breaches between Rome and Constantinople which were all repaired, but left scars, and remained so until the break in 1054.

Despite many troubles, most of Christendom managed to preserve its unity for a thousand years. It was then shattered by the split of the Church into two parts, corresponding with the two Christian empires of the East and the West. (The break was the result of a dispute which was mainly political, in that emperors and politically-minded prelates used an estrangement, which was not really theological, to further their own individual ends.) The two parts became known as the Greek and Latin churches, and rallied under two heads, the Patriarch of Constantinople and the Bishop of Rome, commonly called the Pope. (The Eastern or Greek church had been known as the Orthodox[1] Church since the ninth

[1] Orthodox is a combination of two Greek words meaning right or true opinion, as contrasted to heresy, or the wrong opinion, and was used originally to distinguish the true faith from that held by separated bodies such as the Nestorians and Jacobites.—ED.

century, and by that name it is still known today.) Both
parts of the Church considered the other to be in schism,
and each claimed to be the remnant of the true Church
and its full embodiment.

The Western church, with which we are here concerned,
continued in unity for another five centuries, although during that time a continual series of warnings from a variety
of quarters made it evident that there was much dissatisfaction with certain developments in its governmental structure and in its doctrines, and even with its morals and in-
tegrity, and that reforms must come. When, after repeated
and prolonged protests and warnings, the papal government
(which at that time was despotic) failed to countenance reform—or even the discussion of reform—dissatisfaction broke
out generally and the Western church was plunged into the
chaos of what we now call the Reformation. To the confusion of doctrinal and liturgical differences was added the
contending ambition of princes and nobility, eager to profit
from the occasion for their own temporal advantage. It is
not surprising that the pattern of the Church's life and policy
which was worked out in the heat of bitter struggles and
which is still the design of Christendom today, looks so
derelict and cries out so loud for another reformation. *Ecclesia semper reformanda* (The church must be continually
reformed). It was along with a general upheaval on the
Continent that the Church of England, in despair, severed
its relations with the Pope.

The relations between the Roman Catholic and Anglican
Churches at present obtaining were determined not so much
in Henry VIII's time as in Elizabeth's. The unpleasant history of Henry's reign is too well known to be retold, but for
the sake of clarity, it must be remembered that he was mainly concerned, as many of his predecessors had been, with
wresting from the Pope the temporal power over the Church

in England, rather than with reforming the Church itself. Considering the circumstances, it is not surprising that some of his best advisers, notably Sir Thomas More and Cardinal John Fisher, Bishop of Rochester, felt unable to give their assent to the king's autocratic ambitions. They were both executed, and are, not unreasonably, honored as saints by the Roman Catholic Church.

The Continental demand for reform of the Church and riddance of mediaeval abuses found many supporters in England where it was given practical expression in the reign of the young king Edward VI. Under Archbishop Cranmer the first Prayer Book was compiled and then, after only three years, revised.

In the reign of Mary Tudor the trend was totally reversed: papal authority was resumed as was the Latin mass and all the Roman cultus. The champions of the English reforms were put to death, particularly Archbishop Cranmer, and Bishops Ridley, Latimer, and Hooper who, if and when the Anglican church takes up again the business of "canonization," will certainly be honored by the Church of England as martyrs for the faith. Queen Elizabeth I claimed again the secular authority over the Church in England and restored the reforms made under Edward VI. Neither she nor her ministers had any intention of causing a permanent rift in the Church of Christ, but were bent solely on carrying out in England the reforms which the Church at large had failed to effect, some of which the Council of Trent later acknowledged to be necessary. Trent by no means thought all of the reforms were desirable in England and in the countries of northern Europe; some were not even satisfactorily discussed.

A Roman Catholic might call this an over-simplification of the matter and claim that Elizabeth I forced upon the Church what amounted to a major shift in doctrine and worship, but it must be borne in mind that although the Roman Catholic Church now makes much of the Council of Trent, at the beginning of Elizabeth's reign it must have looked small and helpless and unrepresentative. With the peace and continuity of the Church at stake, Elizabeth and her advisers had no alternative but to take the only course open to them, which was to re-establish the simplified English liturgy of Edward VI's reign and at the same time resist the restoration of mediaeval abuses on the one hand and extreme reformist doctrines on the other.

Soon after the Council of Trent a form of trial of Elizabeth was held in Rome, and in 1570, by the Bull *Regnans in Excelsis*, the Pope formally excommunicated Elizabeth and her successors and absolved all her subjects from their allegiance to her. It is not surprising, therefore, that in the heat of those times, when the Pope was in league with the Emperor and was urging him to send an armed expedition against the British Isles, which he did with the Spanish Armada in 1588, Elizabeth's Parliament enacted penal reprisals against any Englishman who remained loyal to the Pope. Executions did in fact take place and were as brutal as any which had been perpetrated in the opposite interest a few years previously by Mary Tudor. The Bull, unfortunate as it was, and unrepealed as it is, still regulates the formal attitude of the Roman Catholic Church to the Church of England.

The history of the Reformation is a mixture of the sordid and the heroic. Unfortunately many of its wounds are still with us, and the great separation remains, but all who long for the unity of Christ's Church must deliberately put aside the bitterness which engendered the quarrels and must determine never to be the slaves of inherited biases.

The executions of both Tyburn and Smithfield are a disgrace to both Churches. It is not unlikely that in a few years the Roman Catholic Church will canonize some forty martyrs (chiefly Edmund Campion) who perished at Tyburn during Elizabeth's reign: that will indeed be a testing time, and all true believers of both Communions should make sure that a celebration is made of the occasion, not as an anti-Anglican or anti-Roman Catholic bit of propaganda but as a real demonstration of God's judgment on intolerance in all its forms. Let Thomas More and Thomas Cranmer, Nicholas Ridley and Edmund Campion and all their fellow-sufferers of both Churches call shame on all intolerance always and everywhere, and adjure us all to unity in Christ.

One other circumstance which has given rise to much bitterness between the two Communions has been the unhappy oppression by four centuries of successive English governments of the people of Ireland. Roman Catholics in Ireland have identified themselves with the forces of liberation, though in fact not all the nationalist leaders were Roman Catholics. It is not surprising, therefore, that since Roman Catholics in England, and particularly the clergy, are largely of Irish stock the old bias should exist. (In Christian circles it should not even endure.) All disabilities against Roman Catholic citizens were progressively removed in the eighteenth and nineteenth centuries, and a hierarchy, purposely set up by the Vatican in rivalry to the Archbishops and Bishops of the English Church, was renewed in 1850. The effect of *Regnans in Excelsis* remains.

This bit of history, brief as it has been, has been necessary if we are to understand the relations now obtaining between the two Churches. Furthermore, each Church draws different conclusions from the same set of facts. The Roman Catholic Church says of itself that it is the original and now the only true Church, from which all others have broken away; that from the earliest days the Bishop of Rome has been accepted as the visible head of the Church in succession to St. Peter; and the test of Catholicity for any Christian bishop, church, or group is therefore simply the question whether or not he (or it) is in communion with the See of Rome. All other bodies are in schism, are heretical, or both.

The Roman Catholic Church has progressively built up a body of doctrine concerning its divine commission and the primacy of St. Peter and his successors, with which readers will be familiar. Starting with the familiar gospel texts (St. Matthew 16:19, 18:18, 28:18, St. John 20:23, 21:15, Acts 15:28, etc.) she has built upon the primacy allegedly given by Christ to St. Peter the doctrines of Inerrancy of the Church and Infallibility of the Pope, and claims that both are legitimate developments of the original doctrine. Of the Church of England the Roman Catholic Church says that, having thrown out the "old faith" at the Reformation and having started a "new religion," it is not a true church. Of the churches and denominations which derive, at least in some measure, from the Church of England, the same statement would be made. The view is one of theological relevance because it means that the Roman Catholic Church must always and everywhere strive to bring every baptized Christian within its own fold. The Roman Catholic Church is vigorously engaged not only in converting the non-Christian, but also in bringing every non-Roman Catholic Christian to the obedience of the Bishop of Rome. Although on the surface the Roman Catholic Church enjoys a peaceful and courteous coexistence with other Christians, there is nevertheless a subterranean warfare against their independence. "Jesus convert England" is the daily prayer of many loyal Roman Catholics, and a similar prayer is said for other countries, and its purpose is not only to convert the unbeliever but to bring every bishop, priest, deacon, and layman of the Church of England, and in fact every other Christian, into the Roman Catholic fold.

The interpretation by Anglican Churches of the same texts of Scripture and the same facts of history, is quite different. The Anglican Communion has had, and still has, many learned exegetes and historians in its service, and is perhaps outstanding for the width and depth of its scholarship; but it is unable, in all honesty, to agree that the gospel texts cited can bear the interpretation now put upon them by Rome, or that they were ever universally so understood. Moreover Anglican churches would feel obliged, in an argument, to accuse the Roman Catholic Church of manipulating both the meaning of Scripture and the meaning of the Fathers of the Church in support of her doctrines. That authority was given to the Apostles, that the same authority still resides in the Church, that there is one faith committed to the Church to be kept inviolate forever, that there is meant to be one Church, with a visible center of authority and unity, which ought to be restored as soon as possible—to all of these facts Anglican churches would readily attest.

The rest of the Roman concepts, however, they are unable to accept. They consider them to be unwarranted additions to the Catholic faith—unwarranted, that is, because they amount to an inaccurate interpretation of both Holy Scripture and ecclesiastical tradition, and because they do not have the sanction of a properly constituted Ecumenical Council of the whole Church. The Church of England, as does any other Anglican Church, therefore recognizes that the Church, though intended by Christ to be one, is in fact divided, and that the Orthodox as well as Anglican and the Roman portions are parts of the true Church.

That the reformers of the 16th century had every intention of continuing the Church while reforming it, she claims in a general sense, to be evident in the Articles of Religion, in the nature and form of the Book of Common Prayer, and most explicitly in the Preface to the Ordinal attached to that book. The reformers were at great pains to continue in the Church of England both the faith and the ministerial structure of the one, holy, catholic and apostolic Church. Far from having jettisoned the "old faith," she has kept it intact; it is the Roman Catholic Church which has added innovations.

The Anglican Church also recognizes many other bodies of Christians as members of the true Church, so many that in the present confusion she is not prepared to define the limits of inclusion any narrower than to "acknowledge that all those who believe in our Lord Jesus Christ, and have been baptized (with water) and in the name of the Holy Trinity" to be members of the Church. In the present circumstances of division, that is the only possible interpretation she can make, according to Holy Scripture and the tradition of the Fathers: it is, of course, to be distinguished, for example, from the view of some Protestants that the Church is an invisible society, whose members are known only to God.

Such, stated without evidence or argument, are the concepts of the nature of the Church held by the two communions, Roman and Anglican. Both interpretations are capable of further examination: the Church of England could state where authority in the Church really resides, and the Roman Catholics could explain what the eschatological and ecclesiastical status is of those who, though validly baptized, are not in communion with the Bishop of Rome.

There have been indications that both sides are willing to think out the matters which are related; and it is to be hoped that if some of their theologians can be authorized to discuss them together, good may ensue. In the preparatory stages of the Vatican Council there has been clear evidence that the Roman Catholic Church, on her side, intends to tackle the problem.

3

PRESENT RELATIONS:

DOCTRINAL DIFFERENCES

THE events of history, as we have seen, brought the relations between the Roman Catholic Church and the Churches of the Anglican Communion (and all the churches of the Protestant world) to a complete rupture. So deep and so violent a separation is not, of course, caused by events alone, but is founded on severe doctrinal disagreements. This chapter will endeavor to state, again without evidence or argument, the main points of doctrinal disagreement.

For the sake of proportion, and eventually of truth, the reader is asked to bear in mind that points of agreement between the two bodies are far more in number, and far greater in importance, than the ones of disagreement, an indisputable fact to keep firmly in view. It is almost incredible that, in the face of present emergencies, Christian people who agree about so much can be separated by so little.

It is tragic when two bodies who agree, for example, as to the manner and nature of Our Lord's Incarnation should be separated by a disagreement about the nature of His presence in the Eucharist; or, agreeing that His own sacrifice upon the Cross is an atonement for the sins of mankind, they should disagree over the way in which that sacrifice is made effective for man's salvation, or the way in which the Eucharist itself can be called a sacrifice.

The main items of disagreement arise from a difference in concept of the Church, its nature, purpose, and authority. To describe the difference as a radical one is incorrect since most doctrines pertaining to the Church start from the same root.

23

It is the branches which shoot out in different directions. That the Church is a visible body, and that it has authority in matters of faith, is common ground between Anglican Churches and the Church in Rome. But the Roman Catholic Church goes further and claims the Church has a certain hierarchical structure never to be varied; she is infallible, and the seat of authority and infallibility resides with the Bishop of Rome as successor of St. Peter and as "Vicar of Christ on earth." All that is taught as a matter of divine revelation is to be held by all as an essential and invariable part of the Christian faith.

Anglican Churches, in common with the Protestants, are unable to accept the further claims as traceable to the original deposit of faith, or as having been agreed to by universal councils of the Church, still less as having been given by special divine revelation—and therefore must regard them as unwarranted additions to the Catholic faith[1] and impositions upon the consciences of believers.

The promulgation and the propagation of the last-named doctrines by the Roman Catholic Church independently of the rest of Christendom has naturally had far-reaching consequences. The Roman Catholic Church is obviously at a great advantage, practically, in ministering to those many people whose concept of religion is only that of something which should give comfort in this world and assurance of the next. By the strange humor of human conditions she is in the same position, relatively, as those extreme Bible fundamentalists who, on the inerrant text of Holy Scripture (as they hold it to be), offer the assurance of salvation, and in doing so exclude from the company of the faithful those who do not find salvation that particular way.

Even though missionaries of the Roman Catholic Church and the extreme Bible fundamentalist groups (strange com-

[1] Articles of Religion, Articles XIX, XX, and XXI.

panions!) are at the moment the most energetic and effective proselytizers in the world, a large number of Christians are not able to find either one appealing. They believe that a dogmatic concept of authority not only is totally out of tune with Scripture and the tradition of the undivided Church, but is rather a reversion to traditions (they would reluctantly say superstitions) of the pre-Christian era. There are many outside the Roman Catholic Church who might be prepared, for the primacy of the Pope as constitutional administrative authority; further, they would agree that what was clearly intended from the beginning was a conciliar type of authority, properly constituted and generally accepted—a body through which, not by infallible revelations, but by general and steady guidance, the Holy Ghost could lead the Church progressively into all truth.

Meanwhile, the Church, being in a state of disruption and the seat of authority unsure, speaks with uncertain voice. Non-Roman Catholic Christendom is divided, and the Church in Rome has not failed to make use of the fact in her propaganda. Non-Roman Catholic Christians, however, have to point to the violent intellectual opposition to Christianity in all its forms which an uncompromising concept of the Church has provoked in every country where the Roman Catholic Church is dominant. All Christendom languishes, and must languish, until this sticky problem is resolved— all the more reason why all Christians must hope and pray that the forthcoming Council will be rightly guided.

Another difference in doctrine pertains to the matter technically known as the "sources of revelation," that is, Scripture and tradition. A dogmatic concept of the Church's teaching authority has led the Roman Catholic Church to elevate tradition (the teachings of councils and Popes) into a source of revelation equal with Holy Scripture. It was one of the dogmas which had been so misused before the Reformation that it caused many of the Reformers to cast out tradition altogether, and consider Holy Scripture as the only authority in the Church.

The Anglican reformers, remembering the classical objection (If Scripture is authoritative, who is to say authoritatively how it is to be interpreted?), steered the Anglican Church, as usual, into the middle path. Their Articles of Religion, while maintaining the primacy of Scripture, allowed not only a place to councils (when they could be properly constituted) but also to tradition (when it could be rationally considered); both the decrees of councils and the results of tradition were subject to an appeal to Scripture and to revision by subsequent councils. Perhaps the hopes of agreement are higher now than they were at the Reformation.

Since our ideas about biblical interpretation have changed during the last four centuries, we should not now make so sharp a distinction between Scripture and tradition. Scripture, we have come to see, is part of tradition and continuous with it; but, being the fountain-head of *apostolic* tradition, it has a controlling authority over the subsequent development: it is the norm and criterion of apostolicity in doctrinal matters. Hence, as in the great Ecumenical Councils, all formulations of doctrine must be consistent with Holy Scripture and not additional to, or subtractive from, it.

The Roman Catholic interpretation of the teaching office of the Church has had three consequences which have furthered estrangement and incompatibility. The first has been the Roman use of the doctrine of "development"; although it is no new doctrine and has never been precisely defined, it has been used increasingly in the past century, especially since John Henry Newman popularized it in his own particular form. Its proponents would say that it was revealed (its opponents would say it was invented) to handle the difficulties of relating Scripture and tradition.

For example, the doctrines of transubstantiation, or of the bodily assumption of the Blessed Virgin Mary into heaven, though specifically not stated in Holy Scripture, are said by the Roman Catholic Church to be legitimate developments, under revelation, of teachings therein contained. The Church of England, and all other Anglican Churches, as well as all Protestants, would say that they were not legitimate developments but unwarranted additions to the Faith.

The second consequence has been the elaboration of the doctrine-defining machinery of the Roman Catholic Church. The prerogative of defining doctrine and morals has been concentrated in the office of the Pope; and he can, as in the case of the Assumption, do so without calling a Council. For that reason alone it is a matter of thanksgiving that the Second Vatican Council has been called. (Some had feared that the 1870 dogma of infallibility might have put an end to all Roman Catholic councils.)

It is evident that the First Vatican Council, which was hurried by political events and perhaps marred by lack of preparation, isolated the dogma of 1870 from the doctrines of the Church and the episcopate, of which it was intended to form a part. Even so, at its widest, the definition of doctrine is confined absolutely to the hierarchy, the bishops, who are known as the *ecclesia docens*. The clergy and the laity, as such, have no voice in the matter.

The third consequence (of Roman Catholic interpretation of the Church and her teaching office) is that having conceived a dogma she has felt impelled to use it freely in the interests, as she would say, of safeguarding the truth. Her faithful are therefore committed to a series of elaborately detailed definitions of the faith, while Christians outside the See of Rome are allowed considerable liberty of interpretation.

The hierarchy accuses the rest of Christendom of being

vague, self-contradictory, and half-hearted in guarding the faith against misconception. On the other hand, non-Roman Catholics regard themselves as enjoying the "glorious liberty of the children of God" not unlike members of the early Church, whose liberty was continually being spied upon by Judaizing Christians who sought ways to compel them to observe the Mosaic Law in its fulness. The decrees of the first Council of Jerusalem were made in the interest of comprehensiveness and freedom. (May the same be said of the Second Vatican Council!) The tendency to over-elaborate dogma in the Roman Catholic Church is seen from the Anglican point of view, to have the further unhappy consequence of stifling reason (which has its proper place in religion) and encouraging the growth of scepticism. Anglicans would say that the Church in Rome by the course she has pursued, by trials for heresy, by the Index, and so on, has given Christian religion such a bad name that the word dogma is now repugnant.

The Church of England, while quite firmly rejecting the Roman Catholic doctrine of transubstantiation in the sixteenth century, did not at the same time compose a substitute definition. It seemed sufficient to say that the Sacrament was a mystery and that the consecrated elements "are the visible and effective sign of the Body and Blood of our Lord Jesus Christ, verily and indeed received by the faithful." It now seems absurd that bodies who should be united by the common enjoyment of the Sacrament are separated by disputes about the manner of its operation and certain devotional consequences of believing in it.

Another matter of disagreement is found in the Eucharist. The Roman Catholic Church has felt it necessary not only to state the mystery of the Eucharist but also to define or explain the mystery. Anglican Churches hold, no less devoutly, that the Sacrament is indeed a mystery and an effective means of salvation, and that in it the Body and Blood of Christ are truly received, but they do not hold it necessary to define, still less to bind on consciences as a matter of faith, the mode of its happening.

The Roman Catholic Church teaches, as necessary to faith, that the Mass is a sacrifice—a bloodless renewal of the sacrifice of Christ upon the Cross; it is propitiatory, and, like the sacrifice of the Cross, is effective for man's salvation, though it does not detract from the sufficiency of Christ's sacrifice. Anglican doctrine on this point, again, is wide: there is no statement which implies a repetition of the immolation of Christ at Calvary, or the insufficiency of His sacrifice which was offered once for all (there is considerable evidence that modern Roman Catholic writers are coming to a like mind); there is neverthless a sense in which the Book of Common Prayer plainly describes the Eucharist as a sacrifice, but the way is left undefined. On this subject, perhaps more than any other, theologians of various persuasions are drawing closer together and it need not be forever a source of separation and division.

The way in which Christ's one act of redemption is made available for men was the subject of bitter controversy at the Reformation (it was the continuation of an argument which had begun in apostolic times): Is man justified by the faith that is in him, or by what he does? At the Reformation, the Church of England felt bound to throw her weight on the Lutheran side of the argument, and say that whereas it is Christ only who justifies, it is only faith which can apprehend the mystery. She also repudiated the Roman Catholic doctrine of merit, and as in other matters found herself misunderstood.

The Roman Catholic zest for the acquisition of merit by the repetition of prayers, the cultus of saints, indulgences, and so on, is to an Anglican not only quite incomprehensible (here we feel that we can speak for the whole non-Roman Catholic world) but also a grave danger to the souls of men because it deludes them into thinking there are other names "under heaven whereby men may be saved." On the other hand, the consequences of teaching a perverted doctrine of justification (on the ground of faith alone as opposed to the Pauline doctrine of justification on the grounds of God's grace alone, apprehended by faith alone and hence without reference to sanctification in the Church, and to the saving graces of the sacraments) are evident to the Roman Catholic who surveys the life of the Church of England.

The whole non-Roman Catholic world is guilty of allowing people to believe in, and to live by, salvation through works alone, and by failing to protest effectively against the general delusion that "it doesn't matter what you believe as long as you lead a decent life." So great has been the misunderstanding about faith and works that some writers claim that the only possible solution would be to approach the whole subject from a new angle, for example, a consideration of the nature of God's sanctifying grace. There is obviously much scope for exchange of thought and understanding and it is to be hoped again that the Council will find it possible to consider the matter.

Two doctrines which have been defined since Trent and are widely known to be causes of separation are concerned with alleged revelations about the Blessed Virgin Mary: they are the Immaculate Conception and the Assumption, and are only two manifestations of a tendency in the Roman Catholic Church which Anglican Churches (in common with all non-Roman Catholic bodies) find it increasingly difficult to understand. There are, also, the doctrines of *Maria Mediatrix* and *Maria co-Redemptrix*, which are being cherished and pushed for definition. There seems to be no possibility of mutual acceptance of the doctrines as they are presently understood, and the most that can be hoped for is that the Council will not attempt further definitions.

It is also possible that some attempt may be made to grade doctrines in degree of importance. There must presumably be some difference between the anathema which attaches to a man who, although fully honoring the Blessed Virgin Mother of our Lord, feels intellectually unable to give a rational assent to her bodily assumption into heaven, and the anathema which attaches to one who denies the Incarnation of our Lord. Both involve pitting private judgment against the teaching of the Church, but there is clearly a substantial difference between the two.

Some Roman Catholic writers have begun to draw a distinction between peripheral and essential doctrines, but Anglican Churches, again preserving the Catholic instincts of a reasonable comprehension and freedom of interpretation, have attempted no definitions concerning the status of, or any honor due to, our Lord's mother. Although most Anglicans are probably content with the terminology of the Council of Ephesus, they are at liberty to use such devotions to the Blessed Virgin Mary as are consistent with Scripture and the traditions of the Church. In this matter, Roman Catholics would say of Anglicans that they are not comprehensive, lack in devotion, and are involved in heresy. Anglicans, on the other hand, claim to preserve the liberty of the faithful and to resist unnecessary definition.

Mention should also be made of the doctrines of Purgatory and of the Invocation of Saints, which contribute much to the divisions of Christian bodies. The undivided Church was aware of its duty to give man some assurance of his future in the next world by way of encouraging him to do his duty, and to have Christian hope, in this world. The doctrine of Purgatory, which was believed to meet the need, was defined at the Roman Councils of Lyons (1274) and Florence

(1439), and reasserted at Trent. It was rejected by the Reformers.

The Anglican Article XXII rejects the "Romish doctrine of Purgatory," but whether room was left for any other doctrine of the Intermediate State, for which there is justification in Scripture, is not clear. The Roman Catholic mediaeval doctrine had led to such abuses that the reformers of the sixteenth century were glad to jettison the whole subject in order to be rid of it. The same is more or less true of the Invocation of the Saints. In these two cases the Anglican Communion finds itself again in a position of having to criticize the Roman Catholic Church for having over-defined permissible doctrine though it is conscious of having offered the faithful nothing in its place, and of having failed to reconcile the somewhat inadequate references in Scripture to the doctrine of the after-life.[2]

This has happened largely because it has been reluctant to define a doctrine before it was possible for a properly constituted council of the Catholic Church to meet and do so. That is one more situation in which there is much room for mutual edification and which could be improved by representative teams of theologians, if and when they meet.

Another factor in the estrangement of the two Communions is that the Roman Catholic Church does not recognize the orders (the status of duly ordained bishops, priests, and deacons) of Anglican Churches as valid. In fact Anglican orders were solemnly declared to be invalid by Pope Leo XIII in 1896.

The grounds for his action were said to be three: first, that the apostolic succession was broken because Archbishop Parker's consecrators were not themselves validly consecrated;

---

[2] Although formal statements pertaining to the Intermediate State may be lacking, Anglicans nevertheless hold to the doctrine if only because the Prayer Book and Holy Scripture support the same.—ED.

second, that there is evidence of a defect of intention in the minds of the consecrators; and third, that there was for many years a defect of form in the Ordinal itself.

All grounds have been vigorously contested and the arguments refuted. One has only to reread the Preface to the Ordinal in the Prayer Book to see how clearly the Church of England intended to continue, unbroken, the historic ministry of the Catholic Church. The facts of history can be trusted to take care of the rest, though it may be pointed out that even if the validity of order was contested as a result of minute historical investigation, the English succession does not depend solely on the consecration of Archbishop Parker. The matter is not of major importance, but it is hoped that it will one day be revised.

Although the Bull of Leo XIII said that the decision was final, there are happily precedents for reopening a question which Rome has declared closed; the best known of which is the Bull of Clement XIV in 1773 which dissolved the Jesuit order once and for all; Pius VII in 1814 not only reopened the question but reversed the decision of his predecessor.

One of the causes of estrangement, though not technically of division, which is best known today pertains to morals: divorce and remarriage, planned parenthood, and mixed marriages. They are related, in one way or another, to pure doctrine, and in some cases derive directly from it—from the nature of the Church and her authority, the relation of the Church to the world, and natural law. The problems which they bring are not likely to be permanent causes of separation. It is to be hoped, however, that each side will acquaint itself carefully with the beliefs and practice of the other, and perhaps re-examine its own rules and regulations—or the lack of them.

The Church of England, for example, might consider (not

without some shame) the consequences of the utter indiscipline of her lapsed members (the Roman Catholic Church in France is in a similar position): in a mixed marriage can the Roman Catholic clergy rely on the Church of England partner to give the children even a basic Christian education, when statistics show that only one in every twenty of so-called members of the Church of England ever attend church themselves? Is something not to be said in support of the view that it is better for a child to be brought up a Roman Catholic than to be brought up with no religion at all?

On the other hand one might ask the Roman Catholic hierarchy whether it is basically decent and ethical to threaten and to cajole a young not-very-convinced Roman Catholic if she decides to worship the one God in the Church of her bridegroom's allegiance. Once again there is much room for further discussion, for mutual understanding, and above all, for charity.

Another source of irritation is the matter of the Roman Catholic Church's suppression of religious liberties, in, say, Spain. The charges, which are always readily admitted by enlightened authorities cannot be made without some self-examination of the Roman Catholic Church.

It is well for non-Roman Catholic bodies to consider which of them is historically in a position to throw stones and to ask if there are still any sanctions against Roman Catholics in non-Roman Catholic or Protestant countries. It is by no means clear how much blame for the Spanish situation can be laid at the door of the Roman Catholic hierarchy or how far the totalitarian State is using the Church as a vehicle of its oppressive policies. Representation will be made, and received, on this subject at the forthcoming Council. Meanwhile, it should be a matter of prayer that God will strengthen the arm of the enlightened clergy in Spain who are working for improvement.

For two chapters we have raced over great areas of historical and theological territory: this book was originally conceived without them, but it was thought necessary for the reader to see the whole sad situation before considering the Vatican Council as a possible first step in the long process of rehabilitation—not at all unlike a member of a rescue squad who, looking at the ruins of his bombed city, addresses himself to the future. Dismal and difficult as it may seem, the situation is not entirely hopeless.

Of the eight categories of differences between the Churches, we have looked at three (Transubstantiation, the Sacrifice of the Mass, and Justification) which, according to unofficial discussions, open lines of study that, if pursued, can lead to a better understanding. (One of the things which can at least be hoped for from the forthcoming Council is that official means may be found for continuing unofficial approaches which, so far, have borne some fruit.)

Of four others (the nature of the Church, her teaching office, the relation of the Papacy to the rest of the Church, and sources of revelation), it has been made clear that they will at least come up for further "clarification" at the Council. Although the eighth has not been considered a fundamental source of division, it has been made plain that non-Roman Catholic bodies will send memorials stating their points of view (particularly on the questions of mixed marriages and population control) to the Council and that they will be received and considered. The situation is not without hope of improvement.

The ambition of rulers and the excessive zeal of theologians, as well as the prejudices and apathies of the people, have wrought havoc with the unity of the Church; and all Christian people should make a determined effort not to be the slaves of inherited enmities or theological niceties.

The prayers and common sense of ordinary people must

be called in to help—a mighty force in the life of the Church which has been given little notice or encouragement in the government of the Church of England and none at all in the Roman Catholic Church, where laicism is considered a heresy, even though there was a time when emperors presided at councils. One cannot help wishing and praying that Christian men and women everywhere will avail to restore what ambitious politicians and proud clerics have brought to nought. The ordinary Christian of good sense can at least begin that work by turning his back on past animosities and errors and by facing the future with prayer and hope and fairness.

4

COUNCILS IN THE PAST

BEFORE we look at the forthcoming Vatican Council and anticipate its possible results, we should consider the nature of a council as a means of procedure, not government, for that remains in the hands of the bishops. A council is an extraordinary, not a normal, means of doing something. The Church goes on steadily, sometimes for centuries, until some crisis or some unusual circumstance requires the bishops to consider as a body their mutual problems, to restore order, or make some clarification of the traditional teaching of the Church.

The first council of the Church is recorded in the Acts of the Apostles 15:1-29. It met to consider a disciplinary matter: whether or not Gentile Christians should be called upon to observe the details of the Mosaic Law as though they were Jews. St. James, brother of our Lord, presided; and after hearing evidence, particularly St. Peter's experiences among the Gentile Christians, he decided to put no more burdens on the consciences of new converts than were necessary for the exercise of their discipleship.

From then on a series of councils has marked the course of Church history. The Roman Catholic Church numbers twenty of them, but here again we run up against the differences which cause confusion, for different interpretations have been put on the meaning of an ecumenical council, or council of the whole Church. As can be imagined, from the survey of her position in the last two chapters, the Roman Catholic Church's concept is simple enough: there is one Church, and one head of it—the Pope, and a council of the

Church, therefore, is an assembly of those bishops, and only those bishops, who are in communion with the Pope.

The fact that nearly half of Christendom is thus ignored does not prevent the Roman Catholic Church continuing to call a council of the Church ecumenical even though it is only an assembly of her own bishops. By Roman Catholic reckoning there have been twenty councils, and that which is now pending will be the twenty-first. (It is a matter of speculation if the Roman Catholic Church will continue the claim when, as is possible, or may already have happened, she becomes a minority in Christendom.) The Orthodox Church recognizes only the first seven councils as ecumenical; but Anglican Churches have made no official ruling as to how many they recognize, and since they hold the three creeds (Apostles', Athanasian, and Nicene) as having authority they must presumably accept the general authority of the first four councils in which those creeds were defined.[1] Nevertheless, the Articles of the Religion explicitly state that the findings of councils are not by themselves infallible, but are to be tested by Holy Scripture, and that some of them have actually erred.[2]

It is well known that one of the principal causes of the Reformation was the failure of the Western church to call a council to remedy in time the intense dissatisfaction of hundreds of thousands of sincere Christians with the life

[1] C. B. Moss in *The Christian Faith*, Seabury Press, Greenwich, page 86, says: "The six Ecumenical Councils mentioned have always been accepted by the Church of England, both before and since the Reformation; not on the ground that an Ecumenical Council cannot err, but on the ground that these councils did not err in their doctrinal teaching, which has been universally accepted as necessary to the right interpretation of Holy Scripture."—ED.

[2] E. J. Bicknell, in his *Thirty-nine Articles*, David McKay Co., Inc., New York, claims that Article XXI "from first to last (was) aimed at the Council of Trent. The Church of England declared in advance that she did not feel under obligation to accept its decisions."—ED.

and teachings of the Church in the sixteenth century. The maneuvers and hesitations, the vacillations and weaknesses of popes and emperors, to say nothing of the impetuosity of the reformers themselves, caused the great flood to burst its banks and overflow uncontrollably.

In 1545 the Pope at last called together a council at Trent, in the north of Italy, to clean up the mess and to try to repair the ruined walls of Christendom—a superb example of trying to stem a tide after the dike had broken. The circumstances of its calling are not clear: the Church of England and continental Protestants claim that since they were not present to call it ecumenical was absurd, while the Roman Catholic Church says that they were invited but did not come. In any case, the Council of Trent was composed of only those who still acknowledged the Pope as head of the Church. It sat, on and off, for eighteen years.

When the Council began in 1545 only a relatively small number of bishops were present, and most of them were Italian; the bishops whose dioceses were mainly concerned with problems of the Reformation, in Germany, England, and Scandinavia, were all absent. It is not surprising that neither the Church of England nor the Protestant churches then, as now, found themselves able to attach much authority, to its findings. (By way of illustrating the extraordinary Roman Catholic use of the term ecumenical, the Council of Trent is regarded by her as ecumenical from its inception!)

Our aim in this book is not to stir up controversy over arguments which have estranged Christians for so long, but, to be fair, we must give the Roman Catholic Church's view of the matter, for it will be seen that much hangs on its meaning of the word ecumenical. In writing about the forthcoming council, a Roman Catholic says:

> After all the bishops and those entitled have been invited, voting members from various countries must assemble,

under the direction of the proper authority, in such a number that it can be truly said, having regard to the conditions
of the time, that the entire Church is represented. In the
case of doubt whether a Council be ecumenical it belongs
to the Church's teaching office to decide the question as
one of dogmatic fact. An authoritative decision of the kind
cannot make ecumenical what was not already such, but
it can infallibly settle that a council was really ecumenical.[3]

Of the Christological Councils,[4] which were composed
mainly of bishops of the Eastern Church, the same writer
says:

[the two councils of Constantinople] both received ecumenical status through subsequent ratification by the Pope
and agreement of the Western Church.[5]

Anybody who enjoys ordinary rational thinking finds himself
completely baffled by that sort of irrational dogmatism.

The same difficulty arises in all definitions of the Church,
for the Roman Catholic Church is involved in the same
kind of circular argument. If we ask Rome for a definition of
an ecumenical council we are told that it is a conference of
all bishops who are in communion with the Pope; if we ask
on what authority that doctrine is based, we are told that it
is on the authority of the Church, so conceived: which, to
use the language of the cinema, is "where we came in." We
may hope that the forthcoming Vatican Council will face up
to the impossibility of ever reconstituting the authority (and
therefore the unity) of the divided Church on such a wobbly
foundation.

It is admitted that the position of bodies outside the

[3] *The Oecumenical Council, the Church and Christendom*, Archbishop Jaegar of Paderborn, P. J. Kenedy & Sons, New York, page 82.

[4] Because the first four General Councils (which met in 325, 381,
431, and 451) dealt principally with matters pertaining to the Godhead,
Manhood, Person, and Nature of Christ, they are sometimes called the
Christological Councils.—ED.

[5] Jaegar, *op. cit.*, page 47.

Catholic Church, differing among themselves, recognizing no central authority, and having to base their teaching on the "authority of Holy Scripture only" (in the interpretation of which they also differ) is equally unsatisfactory. They do have, however, the advantage of having realized the precariousness of their position, and have at least begun to give it some attention.

The establishment of the World Council of Churches was an important move, a very important one, but it must never make the mistake of calling itself an ecumenical council of the Church, at least while the Roman Catholic Church is not a full and participating member. Although the whole movement for the redefinition of the authority and the reconstitution of unity may or may not be properly called an "ecumenical" movement, it does indicate the rediscovery of a dimension of Christian living which should never have been lost; and it is proceeding on the lines that if you wish to arrive at a truth, you need at least inquire of all those who might be expected to shed some light on it.

To invite to a conference only those who are already known to agree does not seem to be the best way to arrive at the truth. It is better for all concerned that those outside the Roman Catholic Church state clearly that is how its method of procedure appears to them. They look upon the Council of Trent as a pale counterfeit, and its decisions, as far as healing the wounds of the Reformation, seem a pathetically ineffectual attempt. Instead of mending unity, it increased disunity and left non-Roman Catholics to pursue their own individual ways. It is therefore not surprising that so many people find themselves unconvinced by the Roman Catholic claim that authoritarian papacy is a unifying factor in the life of the Church; on the contrary, it seems to them that the papacy has been responsible, in more ways than one, for "our unhappy divisions."

The decrees of the Council of Trent were concerned mainly with the following subjects: (1) Justification (correcting some of the errors of Luther, but by no means answering all his questions); (2) Original sin; (3) The Sacraments, their number and nature; (4) Baptism (against the errors of the Anabaptists); (5) The Eucharist and the Real Presence; (6) Transubstantiation; (7) Penance and the "power of the keys" transmitted through St. Peter; (8) Communicating at the Eucharist in only one kind; (9) The Sacrifice of the Mass; (10) Indulgences (stating only that they were justified and were supported by Holy Scripture). The profession of faith now used by the Roman Catholic Church on solemn occasions begins quite properly with the Nicene Creed, but it adds specifically a declaration of belief in the decrees of the Council of Trent.[6]

We have said that the Council of Trent, failing as it did to understand and deal adequately with the problems of the Reformation, and leaving the non-Roman Catholics no alternatives but to go their own respective ways, was, and remains, a disaster. The Roman Catholic view of the same events would be that, when the impetuosity of the Protestants had wrought such havoc in the unity of Christendom, the Roman Catholic Church had no alternative but to call a council of those who remained loyal to the Pope and to condemn the errors, as they appeared to be, of those who had deserted him.

[6] Of the additional section, sometimes called the Creed of Pope Pius IV, or the "Profession of Faith" (which must be sworn to by every one holding an ecclesiastical office), C. B. Moss says, "Every word of this creed is binding upon every member of the Roman Communion, and is regarded as infallible and irreformable, as if it had been spoken by God Himself. No proposals for reunion could be entertained for a moment, which did not include the acceptance of this creed; it is therefore, probably, the most insuperable of all the barriers to the reunion of Christendom." *The Christian Faith*, Seabury Press, p. 471 —ED.

The harmful results of both the Reformation and the counter-Reformation are still with us, as, happily, are also such blessings as God was able to bestow upon the divided Church, despite the obstinacies and shortcomings of its leaders. Even though the situation which Christians of today inherit is not of our making, we must not, in retelling so many tragic events, be tempted to pride, to boasting, or to recrimination, but rather be moved to penitence. As in so many private instances, penitence for a mistake of the past could be, under God's providence, the gateway to many good things in the future.

The World Council of Churches is not afraid to talk about "the scandal of our divisions," and in doing so realizes that it is passing an adverse judgment on some of the past history of all of its members. Half the Christian world will be watching to see if that feeling is shared by the Second Vatican Council. That many are moved to remorse is well-known: it remains to be seen if their good example will be followed in high places.

There was not another council of the Roman Catholic Church until the year 1869. During the three preceding centuries the Church had reorganized itself and found new strength in the Counter-Reformation, but by the end of the eighteenth century a new threat to her supremacy appeared. The great political and philosophical revolt which in Germany had resulted in the Erklarung, had in France and other countries brought a wave of irreligion and anti-clericalism. By the middle of the nineteenth century the new knowledge was beginning to breed what was to be the scientific materialism of the twentieth. A council of the Roman Catholic Church was called in Rome (the First Vatican Council) to consider the Church's position in relation to those movements and to prescribe any necessary counteractions. (The Council met amidst unusual political unrest.)

As far as the new knowledge was concerned, the Council felt moved to emphasize the supernatural teaching office of the Church as an infallible guide; but there were, however, those who pushed another and more forceful doctrine. The story is well-known, how in a thunderstorm and with the city of Rome itself likely to become a battlefield, the doctrine of papal infallibility was propounded.

No Christian should dismiss the doctrine as so much popery, but take the trouble to learn what the doctrine is, for it stands at the apex of a system of dogmas to which it is intended to be seen as the inevitable conclusion. Christ left to His Church the promise that the Holy Spirit would guide it into all truth; Christ keeps His promises; therefore when a council is convened under the auspices of the Holy Spirit, it is a matter of faith that he will not allow it to err in matters of faith or morals.

The Pope is the head of the Church, not just as an administrative convenience, but because he is divinely appointed to the succession of St. Peter as Christ's vicar on earth. In the Pope is summed up all authority in the Church. Therefore when he speaks ex cathedra (literally from the chair or throne—officially, that is) as Christ's Vicar, the Holy Spirit will surely protect him too from error, at least when he is defining faith or morals. All the more will he be infallible when speaking as the mouthpiece of a council.

But the Pope's authority does not rest on the authority of a council and he can define doctrine on his own account; it is even possible, although unlikely, that he could define a doctrine ex cathedra with the seal of infallibility, without any consultation at all. (In 1950 Pope Pius XII (Eugenio Pacelli) defined the doctrine of the corporal Assumption of the Blessed Virgin Mary. This he did after consultation of certain bishops, but without calling a council.)

The Roman Catholic Church points proudly to the remarkable strengthening and progress which has come to her in the years following the First Vatican Council as a result, she believes, of the courageous stand made for the primacy of God's power in the Church and in her head. Where people are given a visible source of authority, Rome says, doubt is vanquished and people enjoy the truth in peace, in a manner of a confident flock under the vigilance of a good shepherd.

In fact more and more often the Roman Catholic Church is inclined to speak of the Pope in the language which Scripture uses of our Lord and to surround him with a mystery which those outside the Roman Catholic Church find it exceedingly difficult to comprehend—a difficulty not really eased even by the modest demeanor and personal humility of the present holder of the office, Pope John XXIII. To many it seems that the whole Roman Catholic doctrine of the Church and her authority has drifted far from the pattern once delivered to the saints and handed on by the successors of the Apostles.

All readers, however, should bear in mind that the First Vatican Council, which set the seal on what is held to be dogmatic exaggeration, was an incomplete council. With the withdrawal of the French troops and the triumphal entry of the new Italian army into Rome, the Council was indefinitely suspended, and its work was never completed. It was intended that the doctrine of infallibility should be seen as part of a whole body of doctrine concerning the *magisterium ecclesiae* and that the doctrine should be related very carefully, for example, to that of the rights and functions of provincial bishops, or of a council lawfully convened.

Was a bishop now reduced to the status of a provincial agent of the papacy, shorn of all individual authority in matters of faith and morals? Would there never be any further use for a council, now that the Pope was infallible?

The Assumption decree of 1950 gave rise to suspicions that such fears might not be entirely groundless.

The government of the Roman Catholic Church was passing more and more into the hands of the congregations (the administrative departments) of the Vatican. The Congregation of the Holy Office (formerly the Inquisition, of dreadful memory) was giving authoritative interpretations of doctrine and was determining policies. Questions about the Church's attitude to worker-priests, or to new opportunities for ecumenical contacts, were all being referred to one or more powerful departments, in which the dominant influences were nearly all Italians who had spent their whole careers in the administrative service of the Vatican.

When the announcement in 1959 of the Second Vatican Council was made, the news burst upon the whole Roman Catholic world as a great surprise: to those who were satisfied with the old ways, it was unwelcome; to those who hoped for new things, it was cause for great rejoicing. The announcement was made by the Pope on his own authority and without previous consultation with the College of Cardinals, still less with the bishops. Regardless of the feeling of the College of Cardinals, there was a great upsurge of hope and rejoicing among Roman Catholics throughout the world, especially among laymen; the more liberal ones rejoiced particularly that at last a council was to be held, and that the lie had been given to the fear that power had been wrenched forever from the bishops of the Church. The Roman Catholics were not alone in their rejoicing.

That the Council was introduced as having some bearing on the question of the unity of Christians caused a similar rejoicing in circles far outside the Roman Catholic Church. Although it has since been made clear that unity is not the main aim of the Council, but is a by-product which might be hoped for when the Council's work is done, the happy conjunction of the fact of the Council's calling inaugurated in the new era of less strained relations and by a pope of genial personality, has led many to think it worth while to follow the preparations for the Council, and later its work, with considerable attention.

The main purpose of this chapter has been to see the forthcoming council in the light of councils in general, and in particular to see it as the successor of the two previous post-Reformation Councils of the Roman Catholic Church. We have said that a council has been an extraordinary, and not a normal, means of procedure; and that it usually meets only for a special purpose.

It must be seen also that with the whole dogmatic scheme of the Roman Catholic Church in the background there is, or should be, an element of the imponderable and impromptu to be reckoned with; for the Roman Catholic Church holds a "fundamentalist" belief in the inerrancy of councils, and the guidance of the Holy Spirit is such that He is able and liable to take the Council in its deliberations well beyond its agenda *ad libitum*. Although it is right and proper to call a council with certain aims in view and to prepare for it in a knowledgeable manner, yet the Holy Spirit must be allowed to lead the Church "where He listeth" and they are bound to believe that what in fact the Council decides is in detail God's will.

The Second Vatican Council has been called with certain aims in view, but it has also been given, by the Pope himself, a very wide field of operation. It is hoped and prayed that the Holy Spirit will take charge of the great gathering and make known to it a means for healing the hurts of God's people, and every Christian worth the name will wish to join his Roman brethren in praying for the success of the Council; nevertheless those outside the Roman Catholic Church are obliged to state clearly, before the Council begins, how they differ from Rome on the nature of and the place of a council in the life of the Church.

In the case of Anglican Churches those differences are respectfully summed up as follows. First, the Second Vatican Council cannot be considered an ecumenical council, but only a domestic conference of half the Church; second, councils, as past history plainly shows, are not infallible, even when consciously and deliberately put under the patronage of the Holy Ghost (for it is evident from Scripture, to say nothing of experience, that it is possible even for the Church to err); third, the Second Vatican Council will be defective in its machinery and structure even as representing the Roman Church, because it is solely hierarchical, as will be considered in the next chapter; and fourth (though this is only a possible difference, and one which may not occur), in present circumstances God's will for the Church can be satisfactorily done only by Christian bodies who are prepared to make deliberate acts of contrition, penitence, and indeed of reparation, for past misdeeds and misunderstandings.

These considerations are inescapable deductions drawn from the formularies and beliefs of the Church of England and her daughter Churches as part of her inheritance of the faith and order of the Church of God. It is not rash to say that they are also the feelings of all Orthodox and Protestant Christians. That being so, surely the Council of the Church of Rome cannot but listen to them. Although they are critical (we trust not hyper-critical) of the Church of Rome and are voiced on the eve of her council, they are offered nevertheless as friend to Christian friend.

The Church of England, to mention only one Anglican Church, has not officially considered its own economy, at least recently, concerning its fitness to take part in an ecumenical council, but its leaders would, without any doubt at all, be quite prepared to receive criticisms of the Church. The

Anglican Church is certainly in no position to speak by itself for the Church Universal, nor does it attach infallibility to its own conciliar pronouncements; its leaders are dissatisfied with the structure and machinery of church government, with the relations at present obtaining between hierarchy and laity, and are working hard to reform them. The Anglican Church is prepared to look back, with penitence, and sometimes even with shame, on the mistakes of its past history, and to do reparation for them.

One of the more pleasant features of the atmosphere in which the present Council is to meet is the possibility for Christians not under Roman Catholic obedience to say frankly, without offense, what is in their hearts; indeed many will think it an evangelical duty to do so. Such possibility lies in the creation of the new Secretariat for Unity at the Vatican, which exists for that purpose (as well as others), and it is to be hoped, by the time these words appear in print, strong Christian bodies will have taken seriously the Secretariat's description of itself: a body empowered "to receive the wishes and suggestions (of the separated brethren) relating to the Council, to weigh them, and, if need be, to pass them on to other Commissions." The opportunity of suggestion should presumably put upon those who take advantage of it the obligation of studying carefully what the Council has to say and of commending its deliberations to the providence of Almighty God.

5

THE SECOND VATICAN COUNCIL, 1962:
BEGINNINGS AND GENERAL AIMS

THE origins of the Council lay, as we have seen, entirely with the present Pope himself, and are part of a triple plan to hold a synod for the Diocese of Rome, of which the Pope is diocesan, to bring Canon Law up to date, and to hold a council of the Roman Catholic Church. The Council was announced to the Cardinals assembled in the Basilica of St. Paul-Outside-the-Walls, on the feast of the Conversion of St. Paul, 1959. The Pope referred to the manner of its inspiration in his *Motu proprio*, (a pronouncement made on his own responsibility), which was published on Whitsunday 1960:

> We believe it to have been at the bidding of God himself that the idea came to Us, almost immediately after entering upon our Pontificate, of celebrating an ecumenical Council, like the flowering of an unexpected spring. From such a solemn assembly of the sacred hierarchy, gathered around the Roman Pontiff, the Church, the beloved bride of Christ, can derive a new and greater splendour, in these troubled times; and a new hope arises that those who rejoice in the name of Christians, but who are nevertheless separated from this apostolic see, hearing the voice of the divine shepherd, may be able to make their way into the one Church of Christ.[1]

There is no doubt that from the very first the idea of holding a council was associated, in the mind of the Pope, with the unity of Christendom, and through and with it the

[1] *Motu Proprio* "Superno Dei Nutu," Whitsuntide 1960.

peace of the world, for which unity and peace, the renewal of the Church was seen to be an essential preliminary. The order of procedure had already been declared in a previous encyclical:

> The Council is to be celebrated for these special purposes, that the Catholic Faith may increase, that the people may be brought to a new and higher standard of Christian morality and that Church law and discipline may be brought up to date according to the needs and conditions of our times. That will certainly afford a wonderful vision of truth, unity and charity—and I hope it will be a vision which those who are separated from this apostolic see may regard as a gentle invitation to seek and to follow that unity which Jesus Christ implored from His Heavenly Father with such fervent prayers.[2]

Although some commentators have shown a tendency to play down the unity motif in the objectives of the Council (with the laudable intention of disabusing those who supposed that union here and now was seriously to be entertained), there has nevertheless been a tendency to ignore the plain facts of the Pope's originally declared intentions, in which unity was specifically mentioned: the Church was to be renewed in such a way as to make reunion more possible for those who were separated from it.

The encyclical, from which we have just quoted, was the first of the present pontificate, and spelled out much of the background against which the Pope saw the need for a council. The sufferings of the nations could be said to derive mainly from a loss of the truth. The truth was being suppressed or violated in many different ways, by the ambition of politicians, by the greed of soulless industry, by the cynicism of the press, the cinema, the radio, and other agencies of propaganda. It was the Church's duty to make sure that

[2] Encyclical letter, *Ad Petri Cathedram.*

its organization was in such good trim that it was adequately proclaiming the truth, not only the revealed truth about God and the Christian religion, but also the natural truth of reason which is available to all men who do not deliberately run away from it.

Nations are able to recognize the truth when they see it, but Christian truth is now marred by the disunity of Christians. Despite the impeccable unity of the Church around the person of the Pope, there is so much disunity outside her borders that the effect of it is spoiled in the eyes of the world. It is for those reasons that unity is one of the principal aims of the Church in Council; nevertheless unity must not be pursued for its own sake and at any price.

> The peace, therefore, which we must seek and for which we must strive with all our might, must be such, as We said, as does not agree with error or compromise in any way with those who are in error—a peace which shuns all vice. To win this peace men must be prepared to renounce their own advantage and interest for the sake of truth and justice: "Seek ye first the kingdom of God and His righteousness" (St. Matt. 6:33).[3]

There are passages in the encyclical which appear to come close to the conception of unity which those outside the Roman Catholic Church generally hold:

> There are many points which the Church leaves to the discussion of theologians, in that there is no absolute certainly about them, and, as the eminent English writer John Henry Cardinal Newman[4] remarked, such controversies do not disrupt the Church's unity: rather they contribute greatly to a deeper and better understanding of her dogmas. These very differences shed in effect a new light on the Church's teaching, and pave and fortify the ways to the attainment of unity.

[3] *Ibid.*, section 48.

[4] Cf. J. H. Newman, *Difficulties of Anglicans.* Vol. I, p. 261 ff.

There is a saying attributed to various sources and sometimes expressed in different words, but it is nonetheless
true and unassailable. It runs: *In necessariis unitas, in du-
biis libertas, in omnibus caritas.* (Unity in essentials, freedom in uncertainties, in all things charity."[5]

We must not, however, delude ourselves that the Pope has
any idea of unity in mind other than that of organic unity
with the Roman Catholic Church.

Observe. We beg you, that when we lovingly invite you
into the unity of the Church, we are inviting you not to
the home of a stranger, but to your own, your Father's,
house. It belongs to you all.[6]

It was soon found necessary to put a brake on unwarranted
exaggerations about the possibilities thus opened—not among
other religious bodies, but in the sensationally-minded press
of the world. On the day following the issue of *Ad Petri
Cathedram* the Pope said:

The announcement of the Ecumenical Council has given
rise everywhere to most fervent enthusiasm and interest,
although there are not wanting suppositions and conjec-
tures which do not correspond with reality.[7]

Despite all disclaimers and corrections, it remains true that
the Council was conceived with reference to, and is intended
to continue to have relevance to, the subject of the unity of
Christians.

In June, 1960, the Pope declared that the preliminary stage
of the Council was at an end and that positive organized
preparation was to begin immediately. He had already set up
the machinery to do the job, and commissions were formed
to prepare an agenda. First, there was a Central Preparatory

[5] *Ibid.,* 49, 50.

[6] *Ibid.,* 58.

[7] Speech to Preparatory Commission, June 30th, 1959.

Commission to sift the work of subordinate bodies and to present it to the Pope for approval. Then there were ten special commissions: (1) On theological questions, dealing with Holy Scripture, tradition, faith and morals; (2) On bishops and the government of dioceses; (3) On the discipline of clergy and people; (4) On the religious (monastic orders, etc.,); (5) On the discipline of the sacraments; (6) On the liturgy; (7) On clerical study and seminaries; (8) On the Eastern Churches; (9) On missions; (10) On the lay apostolate.

In addition the Pope created three Secretariats: (1) On modern methods of publicity (press, cinema, radio); (2) For promoting Christian unity; (3) Administration and economic. Certain other administration and procedural committees were later added to deal with, for example, the many questions of overlapping which must necessarily arise in discussing such extensive topics.

It may be noticed by readers acquainted with the organizational structure of the Roman Catholic Church that most of the commissions correspond generally in function, and often in name, with congregations already in existence. Membership of the Preparatory Commissions has included at least presidents of the corresponding congregations, but membership of the Preparatory Commission is, in each case, wider and more representative than that of the congregation.

Membership of a congregation is normally confined to cardinals and to a few of the clergy who are usually resident in or near Rome. The Commission will assemble representatives from every nation, for the function of the Commission is very much wider than that of a congregation.

The latter is usually concerned with the administration of laws, rubrics, directives, etc., whose shape is already laid down; the Preparatory Commission is able to consider the revision of any department of the Church, to initiate legislation, and to propose totally new suggestions, which is not part of the work of the corresponding Congregation. Each Commission consists of voting members and consultors, and an attempt has been made to include in each of them persons of wide pastoral experience, scholars, and technical experts in each particular field. Where appropriate the different continents, nations to be, and races are represented as far as possible.

Before the Commissions were constituted a questionnaire was sent to all the bishops in the world who were in communion with the See of Rome: they were asked to address themselves to the great task of renewing the life of the Church, to answer the questions, and, if they wished, to ask questions themselves. Statistics published show that by the end of 1960, 83% of the bishops had returned answers; it should be remembered, however, that some provinces of the Roman Catholic Church in Eastern Europe and Asia, and in certain other parts of the world now lie engulfed under communist duress (they are usually referred to as the bishops of "the Church in Silence").

The results of the questionnaire have been catalogued, analyzed, and submitted to the proper commissions. By the time this book is published they will have been passed on to the Central Preparatory Commission, which will have codified them and prepared them in syllabus form for submission to the Pope for his approval, or disapproval, as the main agenda for the Council. Although it will be possible for any member of the Council eventually to bring forward any item not on the original agenda and to amend or replace existing items, it is thought that the shape of the Council will be determined beforehand.

All of this has brought forth a certain amount of discussion by the press. Some have suggested that, in effect, the Council will already have been held, and its results decided before it even meets; it must be remembered, however, that the Council is entirely at liberty to do what it likes with the prepared agenda, and there is no doubt that the main work will be done, and the main shape given to the decisions, by the Council itself.

Discussion before every great assembly of men is inevitable. Before the First Vatican Council, commentators complained that much confusion was caused because nothing was prepared; this time, because there is preparation, the press is saying it will pre-empt the judgment of the Council! Some say that the preparations are too extensive, others claim that it is not possible to prepare for so great an event in so short a time; but moderation seems to have been achieved. The preparations have taken the better part of two years.

By June 1962 the agenda of the Council was in shape and was circulated to the bishops four months before they were due to assemble. Some thought there was not enough time, others hoped that the Council would not meet until 1963 at the earliest, and still others hoped it might be postponed indefinitely. On the whole the preparations resulted in an intensive and extensive corporate effort to do exactly what their chief had asked—something that any organization could be proud of.

During the early days of the preparation, Archbishop Fisher of Canterbury called on the Pope and later on the President of the Unity Secretariat, Cardinal Béa. The Archbishop's commendable visit had many side lights. One was the revelation that the world needed some enlightenment on the general principles of Church life and polity. Another was that the Roman Catholic Church called the Council ecumenical, and so led some ill-instructed persons to suppose that non-Romans would be invited to the Council itself.

The meeting of the two prelates was not without its share of rumors: one was that Archbishop Fisher had gone to Rome to start up negotiations for unity; one other, originating principally from America, was that the visit represented a hoped-for line-up of all Christian communities against communism, and that the Council itself was to be a trumpet call to a new Crusade, this time against the Hammer and Sickle.

In England there was some attempt to suggest that in going to see the Pope, even more in sending a representative to follow the course of the preparations for the Council, the Archbishop was splitting the Church of England. One of the most satisfying consequences of the visit was the widespread approval it received; indeed, when he returned to England, the Archbishop received from all the Houses of the Church Assembly unanimous acclaim, and evidence abounded that the Church of England was at least willing to hear what the Vatican Council might say.

The Vatican, for its part, was well aware with announcing the forthcoming Council that much speculation and many rumors would be let loose, and these would have to be dealt with; and this the Church, led by the Pope himself, set out to do. A flood of speeches and references, and eventually of books and pamphlets, gave a clear indication not only of what the Pope and his chief collaborators had in mind about the Council, but progressively, something of the hopes, fears, and prognostications of Christian people throughout the world.

The idea which the Roman Catholic Church has been at greatest pains to get across, and which, it says, is of importance for anybody who follows the proceedings from outside, is that the Council is not a "conference" of "delegates" in the ordinary sense of those terms, but is "a solemn act of the highest authority and jurisdiction of the successors of the Apostles, with the successor of St. Peter at the head of them."[8] It is to be considered as a liturgical act rather than

[8] Secretary General of the Council, Press Conference, April 18, 1961.

a meeting, say, of the General Convention of the American Church. Rome says that the Council's effectiveness is guaranteed, and its dogmatic definitions will be infallible, for that very reason. Some of the documents speak of "celebrating" the Council, as one might use that word of the Eucharist, and active participation is therefore possible for only the bishops. Assailed frequently by the question as to what place the laity would have in the working of the Council, Roman Catholic commentators always make it perfectly clear that

> whereas the faithful should take the keenest interest in the proceedings of the Council and will have every opportunity, if they wish to take it, of making suggestions to their bishops before the Council, active participation is only possible for the *ecclesia docens*. The laity should therefore look up to them in reverent silence, praying that the Holy Spirit will illuminate and encourage them in the highest interests of the Church.[9]

The view that the laity should have no effective voice in the affairs of the Church is one which finds very little sympathy outside the Roman Catholic Church. It is fair, however, to say that within the Roman Catholic Church itself there is considerable opposition to such a view, and that the more liberal clergy and laity would like to see the Council modify the sharp distinction between the *ecclesias docens*, the teaching church, and the *ecclesia discens*, the learning church.

The general aim of the forthcoming Council is by no means easy to define in precise terms, but it is perhaps best expressed by the Pope himself:

> The first and immediate aim of the Council is to represent to the world the Church of God in its age-long vigor of life and truth, and with its legislation brought up to date,

9 *Ibid.*

so that it is the better able to fulfil its divine mission in the circumstances of the present time.[10]

In other words, the Council aims at a general renovation and readaptation of the Church to the needs of the present day in any way which may seem appropriate. To show how closely the theme of unity is bound up, at least in the mind of the Pope, with the general success of the Council we have only to look at a later passage in the same speech, in which the Pope said:

> When we have carried out this strenuous task, eliminated everything which could at the human level hinder our rapid progress, then we shall point to the Church in all her splendor, *sine macula et sine ruga* [without spot or wrinkle] and say to all those who are separated from us, "Look brothers, this is the Church of Christ. We have striven to be true to her, to ask the Lord for grace that she may remain forever what He willed. Come, here the way lies open for meeting and for homecoming.[11]

The Pope's words have been given wide publicity, mainly because of the impact of one sentence upon Protestants throughout the world. Although they long for the renovation of the Roman Catholic Church (which they no doubt conceive in very different ways) they unite in disclaiming the idea that the Church on earth can ever have ascribed to it the eschatological language of perfection. Not even the Roman Catholic Church after a Council, nor any Protestant church at the height of its reformed purity, would claim to be a Church "without spot or wrinkle"—certainly not in the biblical sense, still less to offer its perfection to others as an example. Protestants who find the Pope's statement especially difficult must remember that the idea of perfection thus in-

[10] Audience to the General Council of Catholic Action in Italy February 14, 1960.

[11] *Ibid.*

volved is a mystical or general kind and must not be con-
strued as implying any perfection attributed to particular
acts of the Church, still less to individual members of it. It
is the revelation embodied in the very essence of the Church,
the *donum revelationis*, which needs no reform; whereas the
earthly shape and members are subject to all the trials, temp-
tations, changes, and weaknesses of life in this world.

The same issue is involved in the discussion of another
topic concerning the Council; how far it can be considered
a "reformation"? There have been those, of course, who have
suggested that the Roman Catholic Church still has to catch
up with the sixteenth-century Reformation before it can be
in a position to adjust itself to present times. The Roman
Catholic Church has an easy *tu quoque* in its arsenal by re-
minding Protestants that *ecclesia semper reformanda* is a
Protestant principle and that any idea of a "Reformed"
Church is open to the same objection as that which, in this
case, is levelled at Rome: there is no doubt that the churches
of the Reformation, thinking of themselves as reformed have
tended to settle down with a sixteenth-century idea of reformation and are now themselves in need of a second reformation. So it is that both Roman Catholic and "Reformed"
Churches have good reason to discuss together both the
needs and the possibilities of one another's reformation.

Historically the Roman Catholic Church is shy of the very
word "reformation," for two reasons: first, she wishes to
avoid the old controversies of the sixteenth century; and second, she is anxious to safeguard what to her is the precious
and essential belief that since the Church is now, and always has been, the mystical body of Christ Incarnate, it need
never to be reformed. Its members, its institutions and laws,
the language and ceremonial in which its doctrines are enshrined all can be renewed when necessary, but the essential
shape and beliefs of the Church are irreformable. Conse-

quently, words more frequently used are "renewal," "rationalization," "bringing-up-to-date," and so on. The word "reformation" is seldom used, and even then in a limited and nontechnical sense. There are many teachers and commentators who maintain it is impossible to separate or to think separately of these two concepts of the Church. The *dona revelationis* are of course, irreformable, but it is better to say that the Church must undergo continual reformation. The official view of the Council in this matter can be summed up in the words of its Secretary, Monsignor Felice, who, speaking of the counter-Reformation, said that the Council of Trent

> took the correct line of reforming the abuses in the Church and converting its members, without tampering with the unalterable deposit of truth.
> The rightness of their action can be seen by the great blessings which God showered on the Church in that century by raising up a healthy crop of illustrious saints.[12]

Perhaps enough has been said to show the Second Vatican Council has been called with the general intention of renewing the Roman Catholic Church so that it may more effectively meet the needs of the present day, and eventually facilitate Christian unity. Other aims are, as we have seen, the interpretation of moral principles as applied to the problems of the moment, and the revision of Canon Law—the disciplinary code of the Church. The three aims open up an exceptionally wide field for discussion and for legislation.

[12] Lecture on the Aims of the Council, in Rome August 12, 1961, by Msgr. Felice, reported in the *Osservatore Romano*.

6

THE SECOND VATICAN COUNCIL:
THE WORK OF PREPARATION

A S with any large conference, the Second Vatican Council is not without administrative problems, especially in
its preparatory stages. For example, how many people will
participate in the discussions? The bishops, according to
Roman practice, are the "fathers of the Council" and constitute the main body. The number of bishops who might be
expected to assemble was given in November, 1961, as follows:

a. Those present by right of office
(cardinals and diocesan bishops)   1623
b. Those who might be invited
(clerical diplomats, nuncios, apostolic delegates)
Vicars Apostolic, bishops of missionary districts
not yet constituted as dioceses, coadjutor bishops,
and certain heads of religious orders   971

Total   2594

In addition, it is possible that every member might be allowed to bring a secretary and a theological expert, although
it is not to be expected that each will do so. Non-Roman
Catholics might think that a Roman Catholic Council would
be composed strictly of bishops who have the jurisdiction of
certain and defined ecclesiastical areas, as is the case with
Lambeth Conferences, but the Roman Catholic Church, at
least up to the present time, has made a few exceptions to an
otherwise commonly-accepted rule. To begin with, she has
in the past admitted to the order of Cardinal Deacon (and
therefore to membership of the Council) some men not in

episcopal orders, so that it has been possible for people in high places (such as, the President of the Theological Commission, the Prefect of the Holy Office, [Cardinal Ottaviani], and the President of the Unity Secretariat, [Cardinal Béa]) not to have been consecrated bishops. Pope John, however, announced his intention in 1962 of removing the anomaly by advancing to the episcopacy all persons appointed to the rank of cardinal.

There is the further anomaly, as non-Roman Catholics see it, that the Roman Catholic Church uses the episcopal order to confer status without pastoral jurisdiction, as in the case of a priest consecrated bishop in order to fill a diplomatic post. Such persons are customarily consecrated to titular bishoprics, usually suppressed or ancient sees in Asia Minor or Africa, although occasionally there is an overlapping of names with the legitimate sees of the Eastern Churches. (It is to be doubted whether in so doing the Roman Catholic Church is doing what the Church has always done, and intended to do; although other churches would not doubt the validity of such a consecration, they do question its regularity.) A distinction is of course drawn between bishops consecrated to titular sees for the purpose of exercising pastoral jurisdiction in a coadjutorial capacity and from those consecrated for the purpose of diplomatic service. Roman Catholic commentators, however, point out that in their view both curia cardinals and titular bishops consecrated for a diplomatic post hold a pastoral cure—the cardinal sharing in the world-wide cure of souls (for the Pope as head of the Church), and the apostolic delegate, or nuncio, sharing in the corporate episcopate of the country concerned.

The third anomaly, as seen from outside, is in the office of Vicar Apostolic—a bishop exercising jurisdiction in a missionary district where the framework of the hierarchy has not yet been set up. Such bishops, who are bishops indeed and exercise their pastoral ministry in the front lines of the Christian Army, are not members of the Council *by right*, although it has now been decided that they will be included. That makes the outsider question the sovereign status of such bishops in the Roman Catholic Church. (It must be recognized, however, that the removal of the anomaly of non-episcopal cardinals is evidence of an intention to restore the episcopate to its proper shape.)

Moreover, non-Roman Catholic commentators on the constitution and composition of the Council, and indeed not a few Roman Catholic commentators themselves, have felt obliged to point out the preponderance of Italians among the bishops. In spite of an agreement in the Lateran Treaty of 1929 to reduce the number of dioceses in Italy, the average Italian diocese is quite small and the number of bishops exceptionally large: in fact there are nearly 300 dioceses in Italy, with a consequent multiplication of coadjutors, etc. In addition there is also the Vatican's diplomatic corps, and it too is composed largely of Italians. All of which means a disproportionate representation of Italians. (The issue can be clearly seen in a comparison of the Italian island of Sardinia, which is divided into twelve dioceses with two archbishops, with the neighboring French island of Corsica, which is a single diocese.) By the nature of the matter, and because of the expansion of the hierarchy on new continents, the problem is not so acute as it was in previous times.

In addition to the cardinals and bishops, the Council will have in attendance experts in every branch of theology which is likely to come up for discussion, particularly pure theology, biblical studies, liturgy, moral theology, and canon law. They will be called upon to give their opinions, but will not, of course, have the right to vote. Also to be present, but only as observers and guests will be representatives of religious bodies of the world. They will probably be present at all solemn ceremonial sessions, and most plenary sessions, of the Council, although the Council will, of course, retain the right to go into camera (a private or closed meeting) when any confidential or controversial matters are to be discussed.

Much of the business will eventually be transacted by divisional commissions, which will probably have the same names and functions as the preparatory commissions, although they will be entirely newly-formed bodies and different from the preparatory commissions, which will have been dissolved before the Council itself begins. The meetings of the Council will be held in the nave of St. Peter's Basilica, and for the most part the proceedings will be in Latin. By the publication shortly before the Council of the encyclical *Veterum Sapientia* the clergy were recalled to their duty to be familar with the Latin language: it was enjoined that Latin should be kept alive as a conversational language. The Roman Catholic world was somewhat shaken, and many regarded the encyclical as a backward step; to the non-Roman Catholic it was incredible, if not impossible, that an international assembly could effectively discuss its business in the Latin tongue.

It must be borne in mind, however, that Roman Catholic clergy are more familiar with spoken Latin than is commonly supposed: they were instructed in it in their seminaries, and are under obligation daily to celebrate the Liturgy and to recite the Breviary—all in Latin, for the whole of their ministerial lives. In any case language is a great problem for the Roman Catholic Church; even if all members of the Council were conversant with spoken Latin (which is to be doubted) the difficulties afforded by the variety of national pronounciations would be formidable. Those who feel that language is a great barrier to the effectiveness of the Council must bear in mind the difficulties of simultaneous and accurate translation experienced in international assemblies such as the

World Council of Churches and the United Nations. Although some people consider the Latin directive a move on the part of reactionary elements in the Curia[1] to limit discussion in the Council itself, the encylical was not intended to preclude discussion of a greater use of the vernacular in the Liturgy.

The only subject which has been announced as not being allowable for discussion is the celibacy of the priesthood, at least in the Churches of the Latin rite.[2]

The several commissions have been reported as follows:

1. THE THEOLOGICAL COMMISSION.

The first work of the Commission has been to bring up to date the Roman Catholic Church's official "profession of faith" in a form which can be administered as a test of orthodoxy at the beginning of the Council. There will be no question, at that point in the proceedings, of restating old dogmas or of introducing new ones. The formula in use at present is the one prescribed by Pius IV at the Council of Trent and modified in 1877 by Pius IX to include the dogma of the Immaculate Conception of the Blessed Virgin Mary and the definitions of the First Vatican Council, especially the dogma of Papal Infallibility. It was Pius X who ordered in 1910 that the oath, as well as being read, should be subscribed to and accompanied by the anti-modernist oath; to that formula will now have to be added the dogma of the Assumption of the Blessed Virgin Mary which was defined in 1950.

[1] Curia Romana: "The body of congregations, tribunals, and offices through which the Pope governs the Roman Catholic Church."

[2] By the terms of their union with Rome, certain Churches of Eastern Christendom (including the Uniat Churches) were allowed to retain their respective languages, rites, and canon laws, including communion in both kinds and marriage of the clergy. In 1950 the total number of Uniats was estimated to be more than eight million.—ED.

The next matter to which the Commission turned its attention was the two "Channels of Revelation"—scripture and tradition. The official teaching is that Holy Scripture, although it is the word of God, is enshrined in human language, and therefore, because of the imperfections and limitations of human modes of expression, is often in need of more exact interpretation and authoritative explanation, which cannot come from mere men, but only through a body "which has upon it the promise of the continued assistance of the Holy Spirit." We may expect much lively debate on, and further clarification of, the relative functions and importance of the two channels.

The Council is also expected to explain further the doctrine of God as Creator, by way of providing a necessary antidote to the effect of scientific discoveries on the world outlook of ordinary people; and because modern philosophical systems are beginning to question the very possibility of religious and theological truth, the subject of religious truths will also be discussed.

Another subject proposed for treatment is the concept of original sin and what is known as *monogenism* (the belief that all sin is in the physical succession of Adam, because of a common ancestry). The Roman Catholic Church is committed, at present, to a literal interpretation of Rom. 5:12 by a decree of the Council of Trent.

Two more subjects on the official list are the destiny of children who die before baptism (Roman Catholics call it Limbo) and the vicarious sacrifice of Christ (in what way the merits of that sacrifice can be accrued to the benefit of man) a subject which could easily be spread over the whole field of justification and sanctification.

Commentators and official spokesmen of high rank, particularly Cardinal Béa, have predicted the theology of the Church will receive treatment at length, particularly as it affects the status of those outside the Roman Catholic Church. Having abandoned the view that *extra ecclesiam nulla salus* (outside the Church there is no salvation) she is not finding it easy to assess the status of those who, being baptized and in good faith, are loyal to the Church of their birth, upbringing, or conviction. Are they, by baptism, incorporated into the mystical body of Christ, and, if so, to what extent can they be said to enjoy the benefits of that membership? Some people say that Pope Pius XII's encyclical *Mystici Corporis* is still too near in time for the Church safely to essay any further definitions in the matter. Those who are watching the Council from outside are bound to feel that future relationships in Christendom may turn on the way in which the Roman Catholic Church deals, or fails to deal, with the problem.

2. The Commission on Bishops and the Government of Dioceses

The published reports of the proceedings of this preparatory commission give the impression that it has been chiefly concerned with three main problems. The first concerns the relationship of the bishop in his diocese to the central government of the Church. For the most part the relationship of bishops to the Pope has been treated theologically (i.e. dogmatically) by the theological commission, but in practical matters it comes under the Commission on Bishops and the Government of Dioceses.

As we have seen there is a strong movement among commentators to urge the Council to grasp the problem of the real status, rights, and responsibilities of the provincial bishop in a papal church; but even if and when that problem is satisfactorily solved, there remains the question of how, administratively, the relationship is to be organized. Some reformers would like to see some way for national or regional councils of bishops, under the sovereign jurisdiction of Pope and Councils, to regulate their own affairs, and it is felt that too many questions are referred to a Roman Catholic Congregation for decision which might be solved by the diocese itself.

In an international body of the size and complexity of the Roman Catholic Church, such problems are bound to recur and need adjustment. (Orthodox and Anglican Churches are loose confederacies of autonomous episcopal provinces, and each could probably profit from some effective centralization.) Many of her own publicists think that the Roman Catholic Church would profit considerably from some measure of decentralization. That will undoubtedly be one of the issues before the Council, and it will fall to this commission to think out some of the implications of it beforehand.

Another matter brought out in the reports of this commission is the relationship between bishops and the religious orders in their dioceses—a very old problem for the Roman Catholic Church. The great orders, such as the Benedictines, Dominicans, Franciscans, and Jesuits are international bodies of great influence in the Church, and they enjoy a considerable autonomy under their respective generals, but in some parts of the world they outnumber the diocesan clergy, or are so powerful as to put the local diocesan in a position of some embarrassment. Much that is done by religious orders is of direct benefit to the neighborhoods in which they work, but the relationship of secular clergy and members of religious orders both to each other and to the bishop in whose diocese they work clearly need careful attention and regulation.

Mention is also made of the comparative size and organization of dioceses. Bishops of missionary districts, with their men and resources spread over large areas and their opportunities for evangelization so great, are bound to notice the relative smallness of dioceses in some of the European countries and particularly, of course, in Italy. The same problem reflects itself, as we shall see, in the question of the distribution of the clergy over the world itself.

3. THE COMMISSION ON THE RELIGIOUS ORDERS.

This commission will concern itself with the relationships which religious orders think should obtain between the orders and the bishops of the dioceses where they work. The orders see themselves, naturally, as large international organizations to whom certain work has been entrusted by the whole Church, and because they owe obedience to the heads of their orders, they do not, understandably, wish to be under the jurisdiction of the local bishop any more than the progress of their work necessitates.

The commission has listed two other matters: the first is the adaptation of the rules of the various orders to the conditions of modern life. The rule of an order framed to suit the life of a monk in the sixth century era is not necessarily well suited to regulate in every detail the life of a monk in the twentieth century.

The adaptation of the rules (and perhaps the dress?) of the monks and nuns and other kinds of religious may come up for discussion and decision. The question has been asked whether, in view of the shortage of manpower in some new areas of the Church, the contemplatives ought to be asked to reconsider their position—not, with a view to getting them to abandon it, but with the idea of trying to combine it in some way with a pastoral ministry.

Mention has also been made of the uneven distribution of religious houses through the world. It is understandable why most of them should be in Europe and only a few of them in Africa and Asia. The Council may be asked, as a result of the work of this Commission, to see if anything can be done to rectify the uneven distribution of religious houses.

4. THE COMMISSION ON THE DISCIPLINE OF THE SACRAMENTS.

This commission has been careful to say that nothing concerning the substance or the divine institution of the Sacraments will be discussed, for all that was settled "once for all" at the Council of Trent, but the Council will consider their adaption to the needs of the present day. The work of the Commission has been complicated by the fact that sacraments must be considered in three aspects:

(1) theological, and so keep in step with the Holy Office and the Theological Commission.
(2) ceremonial, and so keep in view the deliberations of the Congregation of Rites and the Commission on Liturgy, and
(3) disciplinary, and so keep an eye on any developments in the field of Canon Law.

The Sacraments which have been under consideration up to the time of writing, are Confirmation, Penance, Holy Orders, and Matrimony. Of Confirmation it is reported that some thought has been given to the proper age at which it should be administered: pastoral experience points to an older age, while theological considerations support an earlier one. (Observers outside the Roman Catholic Church will be sorry to hear that the commission has recommended the earlier age.) The commission has also considered the possibility of generally allowing this sacrament to be administered by priests when necessary, especially in mission fields.[3]

The main concern with the Sacrament of Penance seems to have been to make it more easily available in circumstances outside the normal parochial life, and that would entail only rubrical changes and perhaps some adjustments in Canon

[3] In Eastern rites a priest is the ordinary minister of Confirmation; he does, however, use oil consecrated for that purpose by a bishop.—ED.

Law. (The circumstances which are in mind surround industry, holiday centers, camps, and the like.)

In discussions on Holy Orders much attention has been given to the revival of the diaconate in its primitive form as a separate order. The possibility of using married deacons in the mission field (to distribute Holy Communion, to baptize, and to catechize) with no thought of their proceeding to the priesthood, is being seriously explored. Consideration will also be given to the revival of the ancient order of reader as a separate office in the Church.[4]

At the time of writing no indication has been given, at least in the published reports of the commission, of what changes, if any, are contemplated in matters pertaining to the Sacrament of Holy Matrimony. Commentators, however, have made it plain that there are those who hope that the marriage rite will be amended in such a way as to give better expression to its theology, particularly to the truth that the man and woman married are in fact ministers of the sacrament.

The priest gives the Church's blessing and sacramental character to a marriage, but the marriage itself is made by the two parties. That the formula *Ego conjungo vos* said by the priest at a marriage sounds too much like the *Ego baptizo vos* said at a baptism, may effect some change in the marriage ritual. It has been suggested that the new economic circumstances of the present day would be better accommodated if there were an exchange of rings, instead of the use of only one, as is the present custom. The Commission will also deal with the vexed subject of mixed marriages.

[4] The Roman Catholic Church has seven orders: the minor or lay ones are doorkeeper or porter, lector or reader, exorcist, and acolyte; the major or sacred ones are subdeacon, deacon, and priest. The episcopacy is considered a superior order and in a class by itself. Anglican Churches have only the three traditional ones, all sacred: deacon, priest, and bishop.—ED.

5. COMMISSION ON THE DISCIPLINE OF CLERGY AND PEOPLE.

The discipline of clergy and people in reality pertains to one group of people: The *ecclesia discens*, literally anybody not in bishop's orders. The Roman Catholic Church makes a sharp distinction between the bishops (*ecclesia docens*) and all other persons grouped together (*ecclesia discens*).

The most urgent problem which the commission was handed is of the distribution of the clergy. The older dioceses, especially in European countries, are more than well staffed, but missionary districts are greatly understaffed. The chief obstacle to a satisfactory solution is the principle of *incardination*, that is, a priest is normally obliged to stay in the diocese in which he is ordained for the rest of his life, unless canonical permission is given for him to go elsewhere: that can be granted by arrangement between the two bishops concerned or, if a man is required for work in the central offices of the Church, he can be withdrawn by an act of the Holy See, in which case he is said to be withheld "*ad nutum*." Because of past experience, the Church has reason to fear the abuse of *presbyteri vagantes* (wandering, or unattached priests), so that *incardination* is fairly rigidly adhered to; even so, the inelasticity of the Roman Catholic system is now obviously causing trouble, and will need to be reviewed. Another factor which complicates the matter is that in some parts of the world there are more vocations to the religious life than to the secular priesthood, and consequently fewer priests are under the control of the diocesan bishops. The ratio of priests to people now ranges between 1-500 at the best, and 1-11,000 at its worst. There has also been discussion of what is known in the Church of England as the "freehold of the clergy," that is, how extensive are a priest's rights of tenure and the bishop's power to transfer him at will. The problem arises apparently from inequalities in rights of tenure; some priests are too secure in their benefices and some too much at the disposal of their bishops.

The report also deals with the new and varied responsibilities of the parish priest in the face of the complexities and demands of the present world, and emphasizes the utter necessity of all members of the clergy to keep themselves spiritually and physically fit (for the tasks which the ministry lays upon them) by regular spiritual retreats and by a disciplined and well-ordered life.

As for the discipline of the laity, the Commission has considered a revision of (1) the catechism, and (2) the "Five Precepts of the Church." In the Roman Catholic Church, due to the exclusive position of the hierarchy, there is a tendency to think of the laity as the raw material of the Church, and that it is the job of the clergy to mould them into the prescribed pattern by schemes of instruction and pastoral formation. Some of the expressions used may seem strange to those brought up in a more liberal atmosphere, especially where the laity are counted more or less as partners in a common ministry. (We shall see later on that in some parts of the Roman Catholic Church the matter is overdue for serious consideration and correction.) As far as the preparatory commission is concerned we are informed that the Precepts of the Church, which are the rules governing the conduct of the laity, having been recently considered are in no need of further revision. The precepts as they stand are to hear Mass on Sundays and Holy Days of Obligation, to observe the days of fasting and abstinence, to go to confession at least once a year, to receive Holy Communion at least at Easter, to contribute to the support of the clergy, and to refrain from being married during Advent or Lent. Lest Anglicans think that a Roman Catholic layman is held down by a discipline of iron, they have only to compare the discipline of the two Churches. A member of the Church of England, for example, is expected to make his communion "at least three times a year, of which Easter is one"; (The Episcopal Church, Canon 16, defines a member in good standing as one receiving Holy Communion three times a year.) Rome says only once. Furthermore, they should note that although canon law requires a Roman Catholic to go to confession (that means sacramental confession) once a year, he is to do so only if he feels he has any mortal sin to confess, and he himself is the arbiter, in his own conscience, as to whether he has or has not.

6. COMMISSION ON THE LITURGY

Published information concerning the work of the Commission on the Liturgy has not been generous; certainly little has been said about what may come up for consideration at the Council. It is perhaps important for non-Catholic readers to remember that for the Roman Catholic Church, as it is with some Anglicans, the Liturgy is completely central to the whole life of the Church and is the principal function of the Church, completely dovetailed into the whole theological scheme of man's redemption, the focus and heart of all his spiritual existence in this world. (The reformers did not intend to deny the liturgy its central position in the life of the Christian, but rather to restore those other spiritual dimensions which are included under the heading of the "ministry of the word," and to see them related to the liturgy in their proper position.)

The Council will obviously have to consider the work of the Liturgical Reform Movement which has swept through the northern half of Europe, and has restored to the liturgical life of the Roman Catholic Church things which Christians outside her obedience say she has lost, or was in great danger of losing. Because of experience or hearsay, most Protestants picture the Roman Mass as that of a priest mumbling inaudible words in an incomprehensible tongue while the people are preoccupied in private devotions to fill in the time; for a few minutes their attention is called to the consecration of the Bread by the sound of a bell when they are expected to adore Jesus present in the Sacrament while the Host is elevated, and they relapse again into their private devotions by saying the rosary or a litany.

It is now widely known that reformers inside the Roman Catholic Church, totally dissatisfied with the liturgy as handled, have made great efforts to recover a real liturgical spirit. The "Dialogue Mass" in which the people are expected to play a full part, the use of the vernacular, simplified decoration, vestments, and ceremonial, contemporary art and music—all have earned the attention and the admiration of the whole Christian world.

The Council is expected to say how many of the reforms may stay and become the norm of tomorrow. The Council will also have to consider how far the reforms should be urged upon the many areas (chiefly Italy) where so far they have found little acceptance. Official pronouncements have been confined to pointing out that liturgical reform, so called, is not concerned with new discoveries, but in recovering what is good and true in the liturgies of the past, and, rather unconvincingly, that the inspiration has come mainly from the hierarchy. The truth is that the progress of the liturgical movement has all been uphill, that it found its inspiration in the *ecclesia discens*, and that the only really official impetus came from Pope St. Pius X.

Reports are by no means precise as to what is likely to be the outcome of the Council's deliberations, but hints have been dropped about simplified rites, more instruction, direct participation of the faithful, and an expanded lectionary.

Independent commentators have voiced many ideas, and they range from the moderate to the exceedingly radical.

Among the most insistent ones, and coming from many parts of the world, are (1) a demand for great concessions in the use of the vernacular, even that the whole Mass may be said in it, (2) the introduction in some form and in some circumstances of concelebration, large numbers of priests gathered at, say, a clerical conference, and able to enjoy together the benefits of a single Mass instead of having to celebrate separately, (3) the abolition of the introduction to Mass, the *Judica me, Deus*,[5] and the "Last Gospel,"[6] and (4) communion for the faithful in both kinds.

Attention has also been given to the possible reform of the Breviary, the book from which all Roman Catholic priests everywhere must read daily the traditional seven offices, all in Latin.[7] In the stress of modern times, in busy city parishes and in mission fields, circumstances perhaps demand some simplification of the Divine Office.

Liturgical reform is a long and complicated process, as commissions of some non-Roman Catholic churches well know, but it is possible that the Council may lay down at least certain principles of liturgical reform and leave the details to a standing commission.

7. THE COMMISSION ON STUDIES AND SEMINARIES

This Commission has surveyed a wide range of problems, the chief one of which, in almost every part of the world, is a severe shortage of vocations to the priesthood and, what is part of the same problem, the phenomenon that most of the present vocations are to the religious life rather than to

[5] In the Book of Common Prayer, Psalm 43, "Give sentence with me, O God . . ."

[6] St. John 1:1, the first gospel for Christmas Day, Prayer Book, page 97.

[7] Matins and Lauds (which the Roman Breviary regards as one office), Prime, Terce, Sext, None, Vespers, and Compline. See *The Hymnal* 1940, Nos. 157-164, for some Anglican Office hymns.

the secular. The problem of vocations is further aggravated by the fact that, in Italy, for example, of the 43,000 clergy 10,000 are over the age of 60. It will be acknowledged that the seminary system in the Roman Catholic Church is more extensive than it is in any other communion, and that it is not uncommon for a youngster to begin a "pre-seminary" training at the age of eight, so that from an exceedingly early age he is constantly reminded of the possibility of having a vocation to the priesthood. The present difficulties perhaps come partly as a reaction against the seminary system, and partly as a result of the steady growth of irreligion in Roman Catholic countries.

The Roman Catholic Church tries to preserve, as far as she is able, the principle of what she calls "free education"— parents have a right to determine what faith their children shall be taught, even in schools which are financed by the State; and the principle is extended to universities. In many countries the hierarchy has felt compelled to establish separate universities in order to protect students as far as possible from the "acids of modernity."

In some countries, however, and particularly in Germany, there are Roman Catholic faculties in state universities. It is more or less true that the conservative wing of the Roman Catholic Church favors the former, while the progressive wing favors the latter system. One of the tasks of the Preparatory Commission on Studies and Seminaries is to consider the respective merits of the two systems and to regulate their operation in the various countries where they are now followed.

8. The Commission on the Eastern Churches

Most people are perhaps not aware of the complexities of the Churches of Eastern Europe. The greater part of them belong to what is known as the Orthodox group of patriarchates, or provinces, and are the direct and valid successors of the original Church of the East, which included the Patriarchates of Jerusalem, Alexandria, Antioch, and Byzantium, (later called Constantinople, now Istanbul) with which, as time has gone on, have been included others, particularly in the Slavonic lands of Eastern Europe and Russia. Their head is the Ecumenical Patriarch of Constantinople.[8] The great churches of the Eastern Empire, as opposed to that of the Western Empire, look back for their founders to St. John, St. Mark, St. Paul—in fact to almost all the Apostles except St. Peter, and even he is regarded as the first Patriarch of Antioch; some of their great doctors and saints were Athanasius, Anthony, Basil, John Chrysostom, and the two Gregories (Nazianzen and Nyssa). It was from the Eastern Churches that the Church in Rome broke away in 1054.

Since then, unfortunately, the two halves of Christendom have gone their own independent ways. Both sides have redivided, the West more than the East, although the East has certain bodies which have been independent since before the Great Schism, such as the Nestorians, the Armenians, and the Copts; certain bodies inside the fold of the Eastern Church continue in full communion but retain their own rites (often the legacy of old political divisions). Some of the splinters of the Eastern Church, notably the Uniats,[9] have allied themselves with Rome, and the Roman Catholic Church has presumed to establish missions and rival hierarchies in countries traditionally Orthodox.

It is important to remember that the preparatory commission on the Eastern Churches is concerned only with those bodies, either of the Latin rite, or one such as the Uniats (who use their own original liturgy and language), who are

[8] For a listing of the Eastern Churches, see *The Episcopal Church Annual*, Morehouse-Barlow Co., New York.

[9] See note page 66.

in communion with Rome; and when Rome speaks of unity, as she does in the Commission on Eastern Churches, she has in mind, we must assume, only the Orthodox Churches. Rome is well aware that intense and bitter feelings of ancient origin and recent political provocations have lessened possibilities of any immediate rapprochement.

The ordering of her relations with her own small Eastern communities must always clearly be regulated by a desire to show that she knows how to respect the traditions, doctrines, and history of the eastern half of Christendom. Rome recognizes the orders of the Orthodox clergy as valid, and she knows that she has the first seven councils in common with the East; she should be wise enough to see that the Papacy in its absolute and present form involves an institution and a doctrine which the Orthodox Churches will never accept without modification.

Although the preparatory Commission on the Eastern Churches has no authority over the Orthodox Patriarchates, it is, of course, concerned with matters of reunion insofar as they affect Latin Christians. One of the objectives of the Council is to bring up to date the Canon Law of the Latin Churches of the East. The published report of the Commission's proceedings show that the members think there must always be a certain degree of liturgical freedom, but too many different rites create confusion and disunity.

The Commission states that the "oriental patriarchs have no independent *jus liturgicum* (right to legislate on liturgical matters), the only power to exercise this right lying with the Supreme Pontiff and the episcopate in Council." Although the declaration helps one to see how far distant is any hope of rapprochement between the Roman Catholic Church and the Orthodox Churches, it is hoped, however, that the "oriental patriarchs" will accept invitations to send observers to the Council. One of the brighter features of the present situation is that the Ecumenical Patriarch of Constantinople, Athenagoras, is, like Pope John XXIII, a man of wide understanding and broad sympathies; but, the reports rightly say, "it is too soon to talk of a thaw in the relations with the Eastern Churches."

9. The Commission on Missions

It is right for non-Roman Catholic readers to admire the immense thrust of Roman Catholic missions, especially in the last century, and devotion, heroism, and sacrifice of her missionaries which have carried the Gospel to the ends of the earth, and it should be remembered, to keep a just proportion of these matters, that even in new countries where the Church of England and Protestant bodies have been working under British sovereignty, the members of the Roman Catholic Church nearly always heavily outnumber those of all the other Churches put together; it is fair, therefore, to point out that the missionary problems of the Roman Catholic Church are the problems of the whole Christian world.

The most serious problem to which the Commission has addressed itself has been the lack of vocations, a problem which is familiar to all other communions. It must be remembered that the Roman Catholic Church has at her disposal the immense resources of her monastic orders and draws her missionaries from all countries of Europe; she is also building up a native clergy and hierarchy. There is nevertheless a great need of a proportionate distribution of the clergy of the whole world both in Christian and non-Christian countries. There are, as we have seen, other problems: the adaptation of the ecclesiastical machine to its new circumstances, the shape of religious orders in the new countries, their relation to the diocesan clergy, the use of vernacular languages, and so on.

10. COMMISSION ON THE APOSTOLATE OF THE LAITY

The work of this Commission is divided officially into three parts (1) "Catholic Action" and direct apostolate (2) charitable work and (3) social action. Much use has been made of the lay evangelists in France, where their activity among youth and adults is perhaps at its strongest, where they have had the fullest backing of the hierarchy, and where they have been most successfully integrated into the general pastoral work of the Church.

To many non-Roman Catholic Christians the Roman Catholic practice and doctrine with regard to the place of the laity in the Church is exceptionally difficult to understand. According to one statement,

> the government of the Church is entrusted entirely to the hierarchy. The help of the laity consists in giving information and pastoral assistance to the clergy, but in a spirit of intelligent subordination.[10]

Although laymen have no voice in the government of the Church, and no place in the deliberations of the Council, their full cooperation in the active apostolate of the Church is both encouraged and sought: indeed, it is difficult to see how the apostolate can ever be adequately filled without it; but, as in many other aspects of Church life, it is only fair to say that there are new things stirring, that men of liberal ideas are trying to make headway against an official policy which at times seems discouraging, that even now lay organizations in most European countries are growing and have become more vocal, and that congresses of the lay apostolate have been held with no little effect.

11. THE SECRETARIAT FOR UNITY

The preparatory work of the Secretariat has been threefold: first, to prepare for the Council information about the

[10] *Dietro il Portone di Bronzo*, Van Lierde, p. 40.

beliefs and constitutions of the major non-Roman Catholic communions in the various parts of the world; second, to keep non-Roman Catholic Christians informed, as far as possible, about the preparations for the Council, and to encourage them to follow its progress; and third, to arrange for the invitation of guests to the Council, and to determine how, when, and where they may be allowed to see and to hear portions of its proceedings.

It has been repeatedly suggested that the Council give serious thought to continuing the Secretariat, or something like it, and pursue the opportunities for better understanding which will undoubtedly be revealed. Non-Roman Catholic bodies and their representatives have dealt mostly with this Secretariat, and they have been greatly impressed by the courtesies of their reception, by the painstaking thoroughness with which they have been informed of the progress of the Council's preparations, and by the readiness of the Secretariat to receive their suggestions.

12. THE SECRETARIAT FOR THE PRESS, CINEMA, RADIO, TELEVISION

This Secretariat has surveyed the field of communications and noted the powerful means for good, or ill, on the lives of men. It has laid down certain principles of guidance and issued certain warnings against the dangers of their misuse. The discussions have gone on lines more or less similar to those adopted and followed by other churches and communions.

It must be pointed out that most of the Secretariats' work has been confidential, and that the foregoing summary is based on meager statements gleaned from the reports of the several commissions. When the Council assembles, the preparatory commissions will have been dissolved; their places may be taken by other commissions which may or may not have the same functions. In any case, the work of the commissions has been only preparatory: the Council will be free to accept, to amend, or to reject their recommendations as it sees fit.

7

SOME OF THE COMMENTATORS

MOST of the information contained in the foregoing chapters has been obtained from official Vatican publications and the documents and speeches originating with the Pope himself; they may, however, be supplemented with information found in other speeches and publications which have been appearing during the two years of preparation. Not only has the publicity covered a wide field of subjects, but the sources of it have varied greatly from the official to the "radical," and therefore it must be considered rather carefully.

It is understandable that an event which is looked forward to by so many millions of people all over the world has given rise to many speculations and many hopes, and has given unusual opportunities for suggestions, criticisms, and even warnings of every possible description—all of which have to be weighed and valued, in light of their reception by, and influence on, the Council itself.

To begin with, it should be noted that conservative organs of opinion within the Roman Catholic Church have tended to remain silent. The official view of the Council is that since it is under the patronage of the Holy Ghost and since its members will solemnly place themselves in His hands and ask Him for divine guidance, excessive speculation should be discouraged. There are fortunately those who, starting from the same premises and professing the same ends, have felt moved by the same Holy Spirit to declare what is stirring in themselves in order to remove man-made prejudices, to correct mere mistakes, and to prepare the hearts of men the more readily to be receptive to the Holy Spirit.

Chief among the prophets of the Council must be accounted Cardinal Béa himself, one of the Roman Catholic Church's leading scholars, and President of the Secretariat for Unity. The Cardinal has written and spoken about the Council perhaps more than any of his fellow cardinals, and, because of his position and special field, he has been expected to speak mainly of the topics which bear on Christian unity. The Cardinal's pronouncements and prognostications can be taken to indicate the opinions, hopes, and aspirations of a considerable proportion of progressive minded persons in Vatican circles. It would be impossible to give in this space a detailed exposition of the Cardinal's views, but in an international press interview given in Italy they were rather adequately summarized by the Cardinal himself:

1. The Council will have before it all the time the ambition of achieving something not simply for the benefit of Christians and the Church, but of all humanity. The Roman Catholic Church could, for example, lead a very large number to united action in the matter of peace, nuclear armaments, and world hunger.

2. It is essential to make clear that this Council will not be able to take immediate practical steps in the matter of the union of Christians. Yet in the renewal of the Church and the revision of her formularies the object of reunion will be kept closely in view. The Council will probably be able to set up continuation machinery which will be directly helpful to the cause of union.

3. The Roman Catholic Church has much more room for maneuver in the matters of liturgy, canon law, and discipline generally than is commonly supposed. In these fields there will be much which the Council can encourage for discussion with the "separated brethren" fairly soon. But in doctrine they are not able, by the nature of the case, to con-

sider change or compromise. The doctrine is not theirs to change.

4. If I am therefore asked if there is no hope at all of any progress in the matter of doctrine, I do not say there is none. The Council could restate doctrines in the language and thought-forms of the twentieth century, and in terms of these questions which those outside the Roman Catholic Church are particularly interested in.

5. We can start most profitably with considering the status of the baptized who are not members of our Church. In valid baptism a Christian is united mystically to Christ and to his mystical body the Church. He becomes by grace an adopted son of God. Although he fails to accept the full faith of the Church as the Roman Catholic understands it he is nevertheless in some sense a member of the Church. Those who in good faith accept the creed in which they were baptized and are observing the commandments of God are "in the way of salvation."

6. When asked what is the fundamental difference between Roman Catholics and other Christians, I say undoubtedly the nature of the teaching office of the Church. Who guarantees the teaching authority of the Church? With some it is the Scriptures, some say each man's conscience, but with Roman Catholics it is Christ's promise to the Church that the Holy Spirit would lead her into all truth which is the guarantee. This seems an insurmountable obstacle sometimes, but with God all things are possible.

7. Of possible outcomes of the Council, I mention chiefly joint theological and biblical continuation committees. Just as Protestants are coming to see that biblical studies are helping them to modify and to restate their doctrine of predestination, so we all may find that these studies will lead us to new points of agreement. Joint action in social and civic matters is another possibility, as on racial discrimination and on

Christian education. There is no doubt that there was wrong on both sides at the time of the Reformation. When we get together to discuss the present-day consequences of it we should do so in a spirit of deep penitence, and in charity.[1]

Cardinal Béa is among those who are not afraid to admit that the Roman Catholic Church has made mistakes in the past. In an interview with a reporter for a French magazine, and having mainly French Protestants in mind, the Cardinal said:

> The Protestants are not alone responsible for the splitting up of the Church, and we must recognize that they can aspire to salvation on a level footing with Catholics. In a certain manner they are also united to the Church, and we Catholics should do all that we can to foster that unity. Works of charity undertaken together should be a great help to this, as Cullmann has often suggested.[2]

An impartial observer, thinking of the bloody ecclesiastical history of France, cannot resist hoping that the Roman Catholic Church in France and elsewhere will feel able to go much further, and in the long run, make acts and statements of penitence for the past, in which others will be glad to join; but on the principle that half a loaf is better than no bread we should no doubt be thankful that the climate of discussion has changed as much as it has on the Roman Catholic side, and express the hope that Protestants too, in France and elsewhere, are working their hardest for understanding and eventual reconciliation.

Cardinal Béa has been the spokesman of the more adventurous liberals of high authority. At the same time he has been careful to avoid creating illusions and has faithfully

[1] The preceding seven points are from a press interview with Cardinal Béa.

[2] *France Catholique*, June, 1961. (Cullmann is a leading Swiss Protestant theologian.)

presented the situation in a realistic manner. A recurrent theme in his pronouncements and interviews has been that a desire for unity should never allow us to lose sight of truth.

In this respect he supports German Protestants such as Asmussen, who has said, "The hope that Rome and Wittenberg may meet peacefully at the Council will not be helped by making unlawful concessions"; and Professor Bornkamm, President of the Lutheran World Federation, who said, "The way to unity should never ask of anyone the sacrifice of conscientious conviction." The Cardinal has added that "any irenical attempt to level down doctrine would be infidelity to the Church's commission received from our Lord. The more serious and respectable of the separated brethren would not wish to have unity at the expense of truth."

Here he echoes the main thought of the present Archbishop of Canterbury's notable speech to the New Delhi Assembly of the World Council of Churches in which he said that the duties of showing charity, of seeking unity, and of preserving truth must always be observed together and never be allowed to be sacrificed to one another.

The quotations give some idea of the range of Cardinal Béa's thoughts and hopes and why his genial courtesy to and kindly patience with those outside the Roman Catholic Church have been so appreciated and valued in the years of preparation for the Council.

Another prophetic voice which should most certainly be heard is that of the French Dominican, Yves Congar, who has been writing and working in the cause of unity for half a century. The purport of his many books is well-known to "ecumenists" throughout the world: it was focussed on the Council in an article in the French review *Esprit* of December 1961. In it Father Congar is at great pains to show that the Council must be surrounded by prayer, from within and from without, so that the Holy Ghost may be able really to mould its members to His will for the Church.

The need for unity, he says, is urgent and compelling, and it must be made to dominate the Council. While the Church is divided, the modern agnostic is given an easy excuse for not believing—Why should he? Unity can be reasonably expected to be advanced only if the Council is prepared to dig deep into the doctrinal foundations for the Church's whole structure and functions.

The Church must be ready to give up features of her life which are not conducive to progress, or which are a bar to unity. She must be prepared to give up temporal power and influence, and must see to it that her members are present in the places where great power is wielded and wield it, often as laymen, in Christ's name and for the good of all men— which is not always the same as the good of the Church.

According to Father Congar, the form of the Church, its image in the eyes of the world, needs rethinking, especially in its concept of authority. The Church must certainly speak with authority, though that authority must plainly be seen to be Christ's, and not just the Church's own. Her message must be stated simply, laymen must clearly have a hand in the formulation of it, and it must concern the daily affairs of men.

One of the most obvious characteristics of Bible truths, under both Testaments, is that they are, for the most part, immediately apparent to simple people; existing dogmas should therefore be rigorously re-examined to see that they pass a similar test, and should be restated over and over again until the need for them and the truth of them is obvious to the simplest believer.

It is idle, Father Congar says, for Roman Catholics to talk of unity until and unless they are prepared to enter into conversations with the Orthodox and other non-Roman

Catholic Christians with fairmindedness to hear and to understand their positive witness for Christ. When the Roman Catholic Church was represented at the meeting of the executive committee of the World Council of Churches at St. Andrews, Scotland, in 1960, a new era began: let the Vatican Council continue its good work and lead us all forward in that era in which we are certainly meant to live.

Father Congar feels the Roman Catholic Church in its Council must find some new way to confront the Marxist world other than with incomprehensible condemnation. Joseph de Maistre, writing in 1817, asked, "Why have a Council while you have the pillory?" We must get further ahead than that and show that the Church has a positive, and indeed a better, solution to the world's problems—and to the Marxist's questions.

Christian bodies outside the Roman Catholic Church should also have a council or councils for an effective reform of themselves—not just a World Council of Churches—with the purpose of trying to tidy up the Churches and the regions in which they operate. (Here, presumably, Father Congar means, for example, that the Evangelische Kirche of Germany should do something about the extraordinary "church map" of Germany and, to give another example, the Church of England should revise its relations with parliament and immediately at least reconsider, though not necessarily change for the sake of changing, the Articles of Religion and the Book of Common Prayer.)

He draws the attention of his own Church to the dangers of *hieratisme*. The word is incapable of being translated into English, and the closest we can get to it is "clericalism"; but Father Congar means the erratic concept of a hierarchy which claims exclusive and full authority and a monopoly of inspiration. That, he says, is a dangerous anachronism in a world in which "one in every four is a Chinese, one in every three lives under Communism, and in which one Christian in two is not a Roman Catholic." Father Congar is an honored scholar of Church reform and Christian unity.

Another author, whose book, *The Council, Reform and Reunion*,[3] has had the widest circulation of any of the pre-Council publications, is Hans Küng, Professor of Fundamental Theology in the Catholic Theological Faculty of the University of Tübingen. The work was written in Germany and has on the whole the German scene in mind. It may be summarized as follows:

The Roman Catholic Church should not be ashamed of "reformation." Pope Innocent III summarized the Fourth Council of the Lateran in 1215 as *propter reformationem universalis Ecclesiae*. Küng interprets the idea of reformation with a full treatment of the scriptural and patristic concepts and in a way which should be acceptable to all, and so has earned the right to appeal to non-Roman Catholics to "rethink the Reformation," as the Roman Catholic Church is rethinking its position. Protestant concepts of the Church have fossilized, while on the other hand their dogmatic theology has become volatile. He admits that the Roman Catholic Church is only just coming to understand and to appreciate the *religious* motives of the Reformation. How could she possibly have done so in the sixteenth century when, in the midst of all the turmoil, she was trying to preserve the Catholic inheritance of Christendom? He asks for Protestant understanding of the Roman Catholic Church's difficulties at that time, and is ready to admit that she made grievous mistakes. With noticeable delicacy he disagrees with the Pope's concept that after the Council the Church will be "without spot or wrinkle."

Dr. Küng further notes that there are many institutions in the life of the Roman Catholic Church which should be

[3] Sheed and Ward, New York, 1961.

continually examined closely, and deliberately overhauled because they are liable to corruption. He argues that the Roman Catholic Church has been purifying herself gradually and has been growing in the understanding of Protestants, especially in the past century; he hopes that the Council will stimulate such good works.

He sees much possibility of mutual study, particularly in the fields of the episcopate, including, of course, the concept of the papacy, the universal priesthood, the nature of the Church, the place of Mary in Christian devotion, the place of Scriptures and tradition, and especially the subject of religious liberty and tolerance. (As for the last-named matter, he thinks that the restriction of liberties, on all sides, whether in Spain, Italy, or Sweden, should be exposed unmercifully.)

One of Dr. Küng's main hopes for the Council, as far as his own Church is concerned, is that it will bring about some measure of decentralization and give local jurisdiction, under the final authority of the Pope and Councils, to national or regional councils of bishops. Although he is careful to avoid saying so, a redistribution of authority can come only at the expense of the Roman Curia. He hopes for radical changes in the concept and expression (as distinct from the content) of dogma and for a better understanding of the place of the laity in the life of the Church. Of the prospects of Christian unity, he says the Council must be a beginning of new ways of mutual edification. Union can be "neither a Protestant return nor a Catholic capitulation, but a brotherly approach on both sides."

Dr. Küng's adventurous book had, for its German edition, a commendatory preface by the Cardinal Archbishop of Vienna and enjoyed the *imprimatur* of the Ordinary of the Diocese of Rotenburg; the French translation had a preface by Cardinal Lienart, Superior of the Mission de France; but one looks in vain for any ecclesiastical authorization of the

English translation, *The Council, Reform and Reunion*.

Another German commentator whose work on the Council has been translated into English is Lorenz Jaeger, Roman Catholic Archbishop of Paderborn.[4] The English translation has indeed the *Nihil obstat* and *Imprimatur* of the Roman Catholic authorities at Westminster,[5] who are at pains to explain that "they do not necessarily thereby agree with the contents, opinions, or statements expressed." It is generally held that the Roman Catholic hierarchies in Germany, France, Switzerland, and Belgium are less cautious about a new idea than those in England and the United States.

Archbishop Jaeger is a German surveying the German scene, and his thinking is shaped by his knowledge of the Lutherans. The first part of the book gives a brief but useful and succinct survey of the more important Councils. He provides an interesting example of a Roman Catholic expositor trying to make it appear that St. Peter, and not St. James, was the principal figure at the first Apostolic Council, although he does also admit that it was "the apostles and elders" who came together. His explanation of the difference between Roman Catholics and Protestants runs somewhat as follows:

Protestant Christianity understands the Christian dispensation as a promise given in Scripture, the word of God, and as a relationship between the believer and God revealing Himself in His word. The Catholic, however, proceeds from the belief that with the Incarnation of the Logos, a real union was formed between God and man in that the Eternal

4 *Das okumeniscce Konzil, die Kirche und die Christenheit*, Paderborn, 1960. English translation, A. V. Littledale, *The Ecumenical Council, the Church and Christendom*, P. J. Kenedy & Sons, New York, 1961.

5 Westminster Cathedral, the principal Roman Catholic church in England and the seat of the Archbishop of Westminster; not to be mistaken for Westminster Abbey.—ED.

Son of God actually combined in Himself a human and a divine nature by the Hypostatic Union. From the Council of Chalcedon's conception of the Incarnation follow the Catholic ideas of the Church and its offices, the sacraments, grace and justification, as well as Mariology and the veneration of the Saints. The entire Catholic conception of Christianity depends on the belief that at the Incarnation the divine order of being entered our earthly one and set up a new supernatural order of being.

On the other hand Protestant Christianity, while retaining the early Christological beliefs, treats the Incarnation as an isolated event in our salvation which does not become a starting point for constructing a theological system, let alone contribute to any understanding of God's revelation and work of salvation. Revelation here does not mean the setting up of a new order of being in our world but maintains that man is spoken to by God's word and receives salvation as an eschatological promise through his acceptance of this word by faith. From this follow all the other attitudes of the reformers towards grace, justification, merit, the sacraments and, of course, the Church. From this premise it is hardly possible for the Protestant to have any comprehension of what Church and ecclesiastical dignitaries, priesthood and hierarchy, infallible teaching office and apostolic succession mean in Catholicism.[6] The Archbishop acknowledges his influence by a Dutch writer, Van der Pol,[7] whose study on Anglicanism will have appeared shortly before this present work. His comparison of the Roman Catholic and Lutheran points of view leads the reader to remember with thankfulness that at the Reformation, the Church of England, while carrying out considerable ecclesiastical reforms herself, was able to

[6] Jaeger, op. cit., p. 59.
[7] W. H. Van der Pol, Das reformatorische Christentum, Cologne, 1956, p. 259.

steer clear of the excesses of the reformers and to preserve a Catholic doctrine of the Church.

Archbishop Jaeger includes a chapter on Anglicanism which in tone and obvious intention to understand is most welcome. He starts promisingly by saying that "it would be incorrect to describe the Anglicans simply as Protestants,"[8] but later on there are some mistakes of fact which are disappointing, especially so since the Archbishop himself is a member of the Secretariat for Unity. He asserts that "three factors combined to give rise to the Reformation in England: Henry VIII's desire to divorce Catherine of Aragon, the opposition on the part of some of the laity to clerical privileges, and the writings of Martin Luther, which circulated in England from 1521 onwards."[9] The Archbishop makes no mention of Queen Mary Tudor's reign and the full restoration in it, by force, of Roman obedience.

It is difficult to believe that the Archbishop does not see that there were two overriding causes of the Reformation in all lands where it occurred: the first was the deep conviction that the Church had erred grievously concerning the faith, and needed to be recalled to the original and Catholic *depositum fidei*; the second was a deep disgust with the moral corruption and practical helplessness of the papacy, to which the only regrettable alternative in those days seemed to be for each Christian prince to be the guardian, in his own domain, of the faith of his own subjects.

The churches whose separate existence was forced upon them by the circumstances of the Reformation are ready to express dissatisfaction with their present confusion, (which is none of their making) and to admit that Reformation princes and some of their ecclesiastical accomplices committed excesses which match at least some of the misdeeds of the

8 Jaeger, *op. cit.*, p. 152.
9 Jaeger, *op. cit.*, p. 153.

Popes. It should not be too difficult for Roman Catholic apologists to be objective about the tragedy of the Reformation, and to cease blinding themselves to elementary facts.

It is to be hoped that the fathers of the Second Vatican Council will be wiser than their misinformed predecessors of Trent, and that they will meet the disarming admissions of non-Roman Catholic Churches by admitting readily the failures of their own forefathers in the hierarchy.

Archbishop Jaeger refers to the Book of Common Prayer as having been "composed by Cranmer himself."[10] He is undoubtedly acquainted with the times; even so we hope that readers will not be misled by his statement but will remember that most of Cranmer's work consisted not of composition, but of translation into the vernacular—an activity which the Roman Catholic Church herself has been engaged in so profitably in the past twenty-five years, four centuries after Cranmer. The Archbishop does violence to the truth by saying that Anglicans "put forward the Bible as the sole rule of faith" (has he never read the 39 Articles of Religion?). The differences of "wings" and "schools of thought" within the Church of England is much exaggerated—a mistake often made by Roman Catholic commentators who are not in a position to know the facts. Nevertheless, we wish it were more widely known that the Church of England in all its parishes is committed to the same faith, and to the same liturgy. Despite his errors of fact, the Archbishop has clearly made a considerable effort to acquaint himself with the problems; furthermore the ecclesia Anglicana often has only herself to blame when she is misrepresented.

So far the commentators referred to have been of the Roman Catholic Church. There are others, and mention must be made of a volume of essays entitled The Papal

[10] Jaeger, op. cit., p. 153.

Council and the Gospel,[11] a symposium by a group of Lutheran theologians. It is interesting, from an Anglican point of
view, to see how the Lutherans, to whom, in respect of the
Reformation itself, we are so close, yet from whom, because
of our preservation of so much of the Catholic faith, we
are so removed, react to mutual problems. For both, the
"Roman question" is pretty much the same and it need not
be repeated in Lutheran form.

The trumpet call of a new reformation is sounded, and
the hope is expressed that as the first one went practically
unheard at the Councils of Trent and Vatican I, Vatican II
will hear the present one. Justification, Holy Scripture, and
the supremacy of the Word of God are carried as standards
in the front of the procession. One is sometimes tempted to
wonder how much progress has really been made in the in-
tervening four hundred years on the Lutheran side. Is it the
case that *Hier steh ich noch: ich kann noch nichts anders?*
("Here I stand; I can do nought else"). Some, but by no
means all, the essayists seem conscious of Lutheran defects
or anxious to set about reforming themselves. Bishop Dietz-
felbinger of Bavaria gives the fullest treatment to the matter
by saying,

> The protest of the conscience bound to God's word not in-
> frequently evaporated into an individualistic, anti-catholic
> defensive mentality. In the generation of the ecumenical
> movement we ourselves must therefore reflect anew on the
> ecumenical responsibility of the Reformation. We must
> become more conscious that its mission, if it is to be a true
> witness to Christ, must be made in the form of service or
> *diakonia*.[12]

One immediately thinks of a similar thought by which both

[11] *The Papal Council and the Gospel*, edited K. Skytsgaard, Augs-
burg Publishing House, Minneapolis, 1961.
[12] *Ibid*, p. 2.

Pope John and Cardinal Béa have suggested that the primacy of the Pope can be really understood only as a primacy of service in the first instance, of the Pope as *servus servorum Dei* (Servant of the Servants of God). One dares hope that the two lines of thoughts may not be parallel but rather convergent. The idea that the Reformation is a dangerous legacy, capable of corruption, is similar to Küng's quotation from Kierkegaard:

> Surely Protestantism, Lutheranism, is really a corrective: and the result of having made Protestantism into the regulative has caused great confusion.[13]

Lutheran essays agree in saying that Vatican II cannot be regarded as an ecumenical council and that the reunion of Christendom can be accomplished only by a type of council which is entirely new: it must be free to come to any conclusion, and therefore risks are involved. There is no a priori reason why a reunited Church should not be episcopal in constitution, but a place must be found in a real ecumenical council for laymen as representatives of the priesthood of all believers.

Such a council would have to disclaim infallibility from the start, but how that action is to be reconciled with the claim that the council is free is not made clear. The nature of unity on the positive side is not examined in detail, and some divergent notions are put forward. The council would be a loose federation of churches who agreed on fundamentals but agreed to differ on peripherals. (The difficulties of this view and the well-known Roman Catholic arguments against it are not examined in detail.)

Lutherans feel that they must do all they can to encourage the liberals in the Roman Catholic Church, but they admit

[13] *The Journals of Soren Kierkegaard*, ed. and trans. A Dru, Oxford University Press, New York, 1938, p. 509.

that those liberals have a long uphill struggle before them. Objection is raised once more to the concept of the Church after the Council as "without spot or wrinkle," because in the limited sense in which that is true at all, it is as true before the Council as after it.

The writers appreciate the Pope's concern with pastoral matters and hope that he will apply the same interest to doctrinal matters. Rome herself has often been guilty of making, and sometimes of perpetuating, divisions by her doctrines and anathemas. Unless she does something at the Second Vatican Council to improve upon the situation, she will find herself more and more isolated as the rest of Christendom grows together. Professor Skydsgaard, in his own essay, suggests that progress can be made towards Christian unity by the mutual exploration of the doctrines of justification and sanctification, and of the visible and invisible Church.

It is important to remember that the essays, although sponsored by the World Lutheran Federation, are not officially sanctioned documents, but voice the opinions only of the writers. Anglicans might find the essays somewhat lacking in self-criticism, although there are many ideas for which they could stand side by side with the Lutherans.

A review of Lutheran appraisals of the Council would not be complete without some reference to the writings of Professor Edmund Schlink of Heidelberg, who has already been appointed by the German Evangelical Churches as their representative in Rome for the period of preparation. One of the Professor Schlink's most valuable contributions to ecumenical thinking has been his insistence that the judgment on the concept of the Church by the "coming Christ" should dominate all councils. He asks both the World Council of Churches and the Roman Catholic Church to study in detail how far either of them has the right to call themselves ecumenical, to consider carefully the synodical system as it developed before and after Nicaea, and then compare their councils with it.

The claim to ecumenicity of the Assemblies of the World Council of Churches is compromised by the fact that they are formally separated from one another and do not confess the same faith. The only way by which member churches may attain a truly ecumenical council is first to achieve organic union with one another. The claim that the forthcoming council of the Roman Catholic Church is ecumenical is nullified in quite another way: she does not represent, or even wish to represent, the whole of Christendom at her council. The only way for her to make ecumenicity possible is to sit herself down in council with other Christian bodies, and to prepare for union with them.[14]

Even though we have very rapidly reviewed the statements of only a few of the many experts who have expressed themselves, and even though we have found a variety of thoughts, fears, and expectations, it is nevertheless one of the encouraging features of the new era (so hopeful for the future), that all parties, so long as they speak in love, can deliver themselves freely, in the knowledge that they will be heard and weighed with kindly consideration—for which mercy all may give thanks.

[14] Der Kommende Christus und die Kirchlichen Traditionen, Gottingen, 1961. Schlink.

8

CONCLUSION

IN attempting to anticipate responses and reactions to the Second Vatican Council, at least what may be expected outside the Roman Catholic Church itself, known facts and feelings at once spring to mind. The first is that without doubt all Christian people everywhere should find the fact that the Council is to happen at all a welcome one, for both friend and foe of the Roman Catholic Church can have confidence that the Council is inspired by motives similar to those which have called the great block of non-Roman Catholic Christians to discuss, if not seek, Christian union.

Anglican Churches, which this book has had chiefly in mind, will undoubtedly so react; although even within their tolerant and comprehensive ranks there will be some who have not yet learned to regard the Roman Catholic Church as capable of anything good or holy. Nevertheless, the rational and peace-seeking Anglican will prepare himself to study, to think over, and to keep in his prayers the Council and the happy issues which could ensue.

The fact that the Council is to take place at all is a matter for thanksgiving outside the ranks of the Roman Catholic Church for two reasons. The first is that it puts the Roman Catholic Church among the number of those many other Christian bodies who are not satisfied with themselves as they are—and for those who have Christian unity as the ultimate aim, that is enough to begin with. It is the grain of faith, the mustard seed, out of which great fruits, under the tending and watering of God, can grow. The second is that the non-Roman, and for that matter large parts of the Roman

Catholic world, are relieved of the anxiety that the doctrine of papal infallibility might have made it, if not impossible, at least difficult, for a council ever to be called together at all.

It can also be said that non-Roman Catholic Christians can be pleased with the Council's agenda—at least as far as it can be seen at this time. As we have said, the Council has been called to take place in the frame and setting of Christian union, and even if our concepts of union seem to differ, we can and should rejoice that the ultimate goal is a common one. We can be glad that the Secretariat for Christian Unity has been set up and that there is good hope that it may be continued afterwards as a permanent feature of the Roman Catholic Church.

We can be particularly glad that the present Pope, who has given such a new hope to the possibility of union, will himself preside over the Council and guide it in its deliberations and conclusions. We can be thankful, moreover, that the main topics which many of us should have liked to have been discussed (had we been drawing up the list ourselves) are on the proposed agenda: the nature of the Church, the relation of revealed truth and Christian doctrine, the relation of Scripture and tradition as sources of revelation, the position of the papacy in relation to the bishops and to a council, and so on.

Although we wish others could be there to discuss all those things and to speak out of their conviction and experience, we know that those who will be there are aware of the many problems to be faced and of the likely need for further discussion. We can be glad for the persistent rumors that probably no other doctrines will be defined which might widen the gap that already exists between us and them.

We can also be thankful that a hitherto unrevealed feature has been made known, perhaps more so than was intended:

the Roman Catholic Church, unlike what is pictured by so many people—a solid, monolithic, immovable, reactionary body, united by nothing but blind obedience and ungodly fear,—is in fact, like every other healthy organism, throbbing with energy and ready for reform, to say nothing of the not-so-latent rivalries and differences of opinion which exist within.

That is not to say that the forces of reform command anything like a majority (that would be to do violence to the truth and to invite disappointment) but we have discovered that the forces of the new life, which are undoubtedly under the inspiration of the Holy Spirit and which must surely eventually draw the Roman Catholic Church nearer to the rest of us, are stronger than we had thought, and we rejoice that they have been able to speak as boldly as they have against the uncompromising and reactionary forces which oppose them.

The second thing that comes to the mind of the non-Roman Catholic is that we must be bold to speak the truth in love and to declare plainly that there are certain features of the Council which we cannot accept; even so we can be thankful that we can at least express our differences in the full spirit of Christian forbearance and longsuffering.

We say that the Council cannot be considered an ecumenical council in succession of those of the undivided Church, but is a domestic conference of the Roman Catholic Church only. Moreover, we ask our Roman Catholic brethren, in love and good faith, not to be dazzled by the spectacle of unity which the Council will produce: a magnificent and impressive sight it will indeed be, and those who have the privilege of being present will undoubtedly be filled with awe and admiration.

Our Roman Catholic brethren must not forget the great army of Christian bodies outside the Roman Catholic

Church, from the ancient and venerable group of Orthodox Churches, Anglican Churches, and other Catholic bodies, to the many and complex sects and denominations which together now constitute half of Christendom and which are slowly and certainly feeling their way to unity; furthermore it should be remembered that they became separate bodies largely because of the failure of the papacy to preserve unity.

We feel therefore moved to say that the Second Vatican Council must surely be a great turning point in Church history—indeed a "cardinal" moment. For the Church in Council will be in a position to give such a "token for good" to the rest of Christendom that it might affect the future of the whole ecumenical movement; it would have to be, however, an effective and recognizable gesture, sufficient to show those outside that she "means business" in the matter of Christian unity.

We hope it is realized how effective even a small token could be, for by a token most non-Roman Catholic Christians would not have in mind anything like most of the "concessions" mentioned in the Council's published reports: married clergy, vernacular liturgies, communion in both kinds, "explanations" of difficult doctrines, and so on. No one supposes that the Roman Catholic Church will soon say that she has been mistaken in points of doctrine, for she has quite plainly said that she will not do so.

The non-Roman Catholic world, insofar as it has thought out its position towards Rome clearly (and, alas, very few prophets have even tried to prophesy), asks of the Vatican Council at least two things in the matter of doctrine: first, that it will have the grace and good sense to admit that the Roman Catholic Church has been mistaken, and has even erred grievously, in the formulation and expression of her doctrines, sometimes in forms which have invited both heresy and schism; and second, that the Council will encourage the Roman Catholic Church to show herself at least willing to discuss with other Christians the nature and modes of expression of doctrine, even if not the very doctrine itself.

It is widely known outside the Roman Catholic Church that there are many, especially among Rome's better scholars, who realize that there is much room for discussion here; and it is also known that her own scholars are often held back by what looks like a conspiracy of reactionary, and usually old, prelates, who have a totally baseless fear that such a discussion will injure truth: on the contrary, there is much evidence to support the view that free and honest discussion of informed and unbiased people will actually confirm the truth.

We must beg the Council to avoid formulating statements about the Church which stress its divine nature and commission at the expense of the accompanying truth that the Church is composed of sinful men. To say that the Church, after the Council, is to be "without spot or wrinkle" will no doubt cause widespread misunderstanding: at the present time such expressions as penitence and insufficiency, and the misuse of God's grace, would be far more convincing and heartening.

The Anglican Communion has already spoken for itself, and has been at pains to show that it is fully aware of its own opportunities lost, of God's challenge refused, of blindness, and of failure. To speak thus of the Mystical Body of Christ no more weakens the belief that it is the greatest of all earthly mysteries than does the spectacle of the earthly body of Christ, tortured, emaciated, and crucified, lessen His Divinity.

The Council will indeed have abundant opportunity to show to the rest of Christendom what we have ventured to call a "token for good"; there are many fair-minded Christians who would be prepared to respond suitably to such a token, and it would help them immeasurably to recognize and to realize the shape of Catholic Christendom as it once was.

If no such token is forthcoming, and if it seems that the Roman Catholic Church, after all the signs and writings on the wall which have now appeared, is determined relentlessly to pursue an isolationist interpretation of the Mystical Body, the rest of Christendom can then have no choice but to continue unity wherever it can be found. Although, as we have seen, unity is an absolute term, yet in a storm one must make friends where he can find them; in this case, although there is no storm, there are squalls and signs of God's displeasure. It is therefore to be hoped and prayed that the many prophets and visionaries inside the Roman Catholic Church who recognize the danger and the urgency of the present situation will be able to express themselves.

We venture to make, in a spirit of respect and humility, certain other suggestions concerning the work of the Council which we hope will not go unheeded. It was an Anglican doctor of the faith, Bishop Sherlock, who said of the Reformation that it was something like washing a face: it was the same face, but the dirt has been removed. Since it is the definite intention of the Roman Catholic Church to clean and renew and revivify her image of the Church in the eyes of the world, (as far as that process does not involve a denial of truth) we therefore express a hope that the Council will take notice of three matters which undoubtedly deface the image of the Roman Catholic Church in the eyes of other Christian bodies, and (what is more important because it is more damaging to them) in the eyes of those who are untouched by Christ's gospel.

The first is the feeling that the Roman Catholic Church is a danger to the natural liberties of man both politically and intellectually. The knowledge of recent and present alliances contracted with totalitarian governments has had a bad effect on public opinion. Both the ancient universities of Britain, Oxford and Cambridge, have in recent years debated propositions that the Roman Catholic Church's interpretation of religious truth and the nature of dogma involves the enslavement of man's intelligence to an arbitrary and oracular source of origin.

Men point to Spain and say that when the Roman Catholic Church gets the slightest opportunity it "spies out the liberty of the children of God," and cite the arrest of Protestants on the borders of that country for trying to import as a "subversive document," copies of the Gospel According to St. John, and so on. They say, therefore, that the Roman Catholic Church is an enemy of free enquiry, and that where there is smoke there is fire. It would help not only Rome but her friends and admirers if she could make some clear effort to show that such fears are unfounded.

The second matter which we respectfully bring to the attention of the Council is the matter of mixed marriages. There is no doubt that Rome's Canon Law and episcopal directives, which govern the vexed subject, give grave offense, and are widely held to offend against charity. We stress this last point, for those of us outside the Roman Catholic Church who try to understand her have to give up the struggle when acts of harshness are repeatedly brought to our notice. Pleas for charity will be futile, unless Rome modifies her rules and regulations.

The third matter which affects the image of the Roman Catholic Church in the eyes of the world pertains to the undue veneration given to the Blessed Virgin Mary. There is no doubt that Roman doctrines about our Lord's mother are often misrepresented and grievously misunderstood; but it is equally true that a large number of learned, devout, and well-meaning Christians hold that the place which Rome now gives to Christ's mother usurps His own place as the sole center of men's devotions—their only Mediator and Advocate.

What is seen and heard and read, shrines and cults, Marian months, innumerable acts of enthusiasm and piety, all taken together, create a false image of the Church and give the impression that all proportion has been lost; consequently, much of the world undoubtedly gets the idea that the Roman Catholic Church believes that salvation consists in securing the intercessions of Mary and the saints. It is not therefore really surprising to find missionaries of an extreme fundamentalist nature, armed with nothing but the Bible and a strong conviction of salvation in the Name of Christ alone, pouring into Roman Catholic lands to redeem, what seems to them, the imbalance of the Christian religion—all to the confusion and defeat of Christian unity.

When people go to the length, even for propaganda pur poses, of dividing the Christian world into "Christian" and "Marian" sections, the image of the Roman Catholic Church has obviously become so distorted that exaggerations, however devout and well-meaning, must be stopped.

We hope that the Vatican Council will consider these three matters, and that its deliberations will result in a new and better and more helpful image of the Roman Catholic Church.

Any Christian who hopes for improvements in the Roman Catholic Church, and thus far has agreed with the opinions herein expressed, must turn the same light of criticism upon himself and upon his own church. For under the searching light of God's omniscience who shall stand blameless? We must therefore take notice of the criticisms which Rome has levelled at us and see if they offer opportunities for reform and improvement. Although this is being written from within the Church of England, and with the whole Anglican

Communion in mind, other Christians will no doubt be able to find the book speaking to them also.

First off, the Roman Catholic Church accuses us, as well as others, of being in hopeless disunion among ourselves, and of having caused, by our own failures and shortcomings, numerous schisms and divisions in the Church. That accusation we must take on the chin. Just as the Western church in the eleventh century and the Roman Catholic Church in the sixteenth helped bring about divisions of Christendom, so, to take the example of England alone, the English church aided the defection of the Methodists in the eighteenth century and some of her God-sent reformers of the Oxford Movement in the nineteenth century. Just as we hope that the Roman Catholic attitude towards us will not be "You are welcome to return to the house you left, just as you left it, without any change," so do we hope that any Anglican Church will not dare to expect those separated from her to return to her, just as she is—unreformed. Anglican Churches can, however, claim that they have already entered into practical schemes for rejoining her separated brethren and are actively pursuing further schemes for mending some of the breaks in Christendom in the British Isles and the United States—but, it must be pointed out, not without some feeling of venture and risk.

The second criticism most commonly levelled by the Roman Catholic Church at the Anglican Communion is that it is vague and indecisive in its teaching and practice and speaks without recognizable authority. It is too frequently possible, we are told, to find, for example, authorized, commissioned teachers of the Church of England sponsoring divergent or even contradictory views in public.

That we admit—but only in part. There is no doubt that Anglican Churches develop much weakness and dissipate much valuable energy by allowing the continuance of "schools of thought" long beyond their usefulness. Both the "evangelical" and the "catholic" emphasis in Anglican Churches have derived from times when prophets, such as Wesley or Pusey, were raised up to remind, in this case, the Church of England, of some great dimension of Christian life which she was in danger of losing.

It should be evident to all that the Church must be always and everywhere both evangelical and catholic, and that to emphasize either characteristic at the expense of the other is to invite weakness or even disaster. That is not to say that the Church of England, for example, should aim at a reform in which the extremes merged themselves into a colorless and insipid compromise, but rather that she should play down their partisanship in order to present clearly the common life and message which has been there all the time.

However partisanship may affect the Church's ministrations, all her ministers and all her people are pledged to confess the same Catholic creeds and to worship God according to the same formulas. There is no doubt, admittedly, that both the Thirty-nine Articles of Religion and the English Book of Common Prayer are respectively overdue for restatement and revision, but the liberty they allow is often taken as an excuse for license; and that leads to the confusion of the people and creates a propagandistic advantage for those who, like the Roman Catholic Church are watching Anglican weaknesses.

Having admitted that much, we are in a somewhat better position to voice some counter-pleas against the charge of vagueness. To continue with the same example, brethren of the Roman Catholic Church are apt to over-emphasize the vagaries of Anglican Church teaching and practice, and are perhaps unaware of the amount of uniformity which does exist despite the apparent divergences.

Rome herself is by no means so uniform in doctrine or in

practice as she once was. There is, for example, a good deal of difference between the Mass celebrated inaudibly, in Latin, by an Italian cardinal, facing east, in a Spanish chasuble, and another celebrated in France, by a priest of the Mission de France, largely in the vernacular, facing west, in a modern chasuble; yet it is the same faith, and the same Mass. The same is true, roughly, of the "High Church" and the "Low Church" celebrations in the Church of England.

It must also be remembered that *on principle* the Church of England allows a considerably greater liberty of interpretation of the one Catholic faith, to all its members, even though some manage to take advantage of that liberty. She considers, rightly or wrongly, that one heretical bishop in half a century is a price worth paying for the freedom of expression which all may enjoy. She interprets catholicity as meaning, among other things, a tendency to comprehend many shades of opinion and varieties of practice under the one family roof—as opposed to a disposition which sets up its own subjective preferences as "universal" and then rigidly excludes from its communion all those who do not conform to them. Nevertheless it remains true that Anglicans as a whole should do more to create an impression of solidarity and loyalty than they do at the present time.

The third charge which our Roman Catholic brethren often level at us in the Church of England is that the religion of the average member becomes in effect nothing more than the "English way of life," (and for the American Episcopalian, but to a lesser degree, the "American way of life") and that it is too nationalistic. Here again, part of the charge must be admitted and part refused.

The Church of England has been accused of being the "Conservative party at prayer." We have to admit that there is something in the charge; but, having done so, we should fire off our answering rounds: first, the charge can apply only

to the provinces of Canterbury and York, which are but
two of the many provinces of the Anglican Communion;
second, the charge is much less true than it used to be; third,
there is much in the Roman Catholic life and practice, say,
in Italy, which seems to amount to nothing more or less than
the adoption of the "Italian way of life"—Italian customs and
superstitions and so on; and fourth, the Anglican instinct,
which, incidentally, used to be the Roman Catholic instinct,
of sanctifying what is best in national customs, has the advantage of making national temperaments more amenable to
the influences of religion, instead of provoking the gross anti-
clericalism which is so prevalent in countries where Roman
Catholicism is dominant.

Another charge which the Roman Catholic Church levels
at the Church of England, as well as at Protestant bodies
generally, is that she does not succeed in teaching her members to regard the Church in any sense as divine, or membership to entail anything more than a casual obligation.
Those who minister for the Church of England know how
painfully true that charge can be, how disloyal her members
sometimes are, and how they neglect their most elementary
duties to the Church. They know how the English layman
attempts to use the Church when and how it suits him on
certain occasions in his life—marriages and burials, for example—and shows no other interest in the Church and her
affairs. We know how congregations and parishes can rise or
fall according to how well they "like the Vicar"—as if worship had no claim upon them for itself, and as though it were
not the Lord Himself who, in season and out of season, was
the object of their worship. In that matter, admittedly, the
Church of England can show up poorly with her Roman
Catholic neighbors in England.

To be fair, however, such a comparison would have to be
extended to include the Roman Catholic Church in France,

in Italy, or in Spain, where large numbers of people, perhaps the majority of the populations, are estranged not only from the Church but from religion altogether. Only then is it possible to make a fair comparison of the problems of the two long-established Churches. (It might be to the advantage and profit of both Churches to exchange views on new pastoral methods and mutual problems. The daughter provinces of the Church of England overseas, like the Roman Catholic community in England, are more alive to their responsibilities than is the "Mother" Church.) It is becoming more and more apparent that Roman Catholic and Anglican Churches have much to teach one another, and that both are defective and delinquent in their respective spheres.

The calling of the Second Vatican Council should provide all Christians with a singular opportunity to ask for the grace of self-criticism, that their eyes may be opened to their own faults and shortcomings, and that they may have the vision to see and to profit from what is good and admirable in the life of others.

Let Anglicans therefore not hesitate to admire in the Roman Catholic Church those things which constitute her glory—those gifts with which God Himself has so conspicuously endowed her. And, let us not forget, that when we speak of the Roman Catholic Church we are in effect speaking of half of Christendom, and not some sect or "denomination." Let us admire her discipline, her uniformity, her boldness in proclaiming what she considers to be the Gospel, her unwillingness to compromise what she considers essential truths, and the sacrifices which she makes in the Name and service of the one Lord in every corner of the world. We shall then be in a better position to raise our protest against her manner of interpreting the truth, her narrow concept of the one flock of Christ, and her mistakes which, we believe, have been the main causes of the divisions of Christendom.

Finally (and this is essential), both Roman Catholics and non-Roman Catholics should ask what is really to be the outcome of the Council, and, further, what each imagines the future path of reunion will be. Do we expect the Pope to become an Anglican, or a Lutheran, or a Presbyterian? Does the Roman Catholic Church seriously expect the rest of Christendom, as presently constituted, to "give in"—to accept the papacy and the later Roman doctrines, as being part of the faith revealed to the Apostles? If not, it is from that very point that our serious thinking should have its beginning.

It is also essential for non-Roman Catholics to know that from the forthcoming Council nothing can issue which in any way may be regarded as a compromise of doctrine on the part of the Roman Catholic Church, and likewise essential for Roman Catholics to know is that there is no possibility of "separated brethren" ever joining her as she is—without reform or modification. It is even more important for both sides to see that the situation, though unpromising, is in no sense hopeless, for as the Pope and others have often quoted, "With God all things are possible."

What therefore seems to be possible? We can see at least four things: first, the Council will give a fresh interpretation to the doctrine of the Church which may have special meaning for those Christians who through their baptism are members of the Body of Christ but outside the Roman Catholic Communion; second, there may be a restatement of some of the dogmas, including that of papal infallibility, which may bring them more in line with the thinking of other Christian bodies; third, it will at least be made possible for Roman Catholic and non-Roman Catholic theologians to meet and consider problems together, and to publish their findings; fourth, the Secretariat for Unity may be continued in such a form as to make possible the continuation of formal relations between one half of Christendom and the other. If those four possibilities become realities as a result of the Council, then it may be said that progress has been made.

As for those outside the Roman Catholic Church, they should look upon the Roman Catholic Church as a *positive* factor in Christendom, and at the same time take up the challenge which the very existence of the Roman Catholic Church offers them: they are said to be divided—let them find unity; they are said to be vague and indecisive—let them show the world that they have a common creed, acceptable to reasonable men who are seeking after God; they are said to have no discipline—let them show the Roman Catholic Church that they can think and act as one because they have the same Shepherd—not an earthly vicar, but Christ Himself; they are said to have invalid orders and inadequate sacraments—let them show that "God is able of these stones to raise up sons unto Abraham," and that through the sacraments which they have, Catholic, scriptural, and free, God dispenses His unspeakable gifts.

If a realistic, intelligible, and humble exchange of thought can be made at official levels (in the spirit in which it has been happily achieved in individual encounters), the Second Vatican Council has promise of being a great turning point in Church history and the beginning of the end of schisms.

Let all those who "Love our Lord Jesus Christ in sincerity" pray for God's blessing on Pope John and all his brethren of the Roman Catholic obedience, and address to their Lord, and ours, the prayer

> O LORD Jesus Christ, who saidst unto thine Apostles, Peace I leave with you, my peace I give unto you; Regard not our sins, but the faith of thy Church; and grant to it that peace and unity which is according to thy will, who livest and reignest with the Father and the Holy Ghost, one God, world without end. Amen.